Caring for someone in their own home

A handbook for friends and family

Helen Howard

To Eunice Armstrong (my Mum)
for refusing to become a 'little old lady'

© Helen Howard 2004
Published by Age Concern England
1268 London Road
London SW16 4ER

First published 2004

Editor Gillian Clarke
Production Vinnette Marshall
Design and typesetting GreenGate Publishing Services
Printed in Great Britain by Bell & Bain Ltd, Glasgow

A catalogue record for this book is available from the British Library
ISBN 0–86242–362–7

Although every effort has been made to check the accuracy of material contained in this publication, Age Concern England, Carers UK and the author cannot accept any legal responsibility or liability for any errors or omissions that may be made. Please note that, whilst the agencies or products mentioned in this book are known to Age Concern England and Carers UK, inclusion here does not constitute a recommendation by Age Concern England or Carers UK for any particular product, agency, service or publication.

Contents

About the author

Helen Howard has worked in health, social services, education and the voluntary sector. She currently works freelance in a range of capacities, including writing open learning materials, e-learning, training packs and textbooks. She undertakes consultancy and project work, particularly in the public and voluntary sectors, and teaches *K100, Understanding Health and Social Care* for the Open University. She is consultant to Anglia Polytechnic University in the development of the Award in the Regulation of Health and Social Care for National Care Standards Commission inspectors. Helen is also a member of the Board of Directors of East Kent Cyrenians, an organisation that provides accommodation and resettlement services to single homeless people, and one of the new Patient Forums.

Helen has written other publications for Age Concern Books: *The Care Assistant's Handbook* and three training packs *Setting the Scene, The Principles of Care* and *Cross Cultural Care*.

Acknowledgements

I thank the following individuals and organisations very much for their help in writing this book:

Sarah Bleach at Carers UK
Helen Cooke
Alison Eamer
Chris and Cheryl Ives
Alan Kidd
David Meredith
Bill Peppiatt MBE
Rethink
Nia Taylor at BackCare

We are very grateful to Carers UK for their support for the project and thank BackCare for permission to draw on their publication *Safer Handling of People in the Community* for general advice on moving and handling people.

Introduction

Who this book is for

This book is for anyone who looks after a friend or relative or neighbour at home in a voluntary capacity. Care workers working in more formal settings – eg day centres or care homes – may find the book useful too, because it will help them to see the world from a carer's perspective. Our focus is mainly, but not exclusively, on older people either as carers or as people being cared for.

People often say that Britain is not a caring society and we don't look after our older people, but figures drawn from the 2000 General Household Survey suggest that one person in eight is a carer. Recent policy statements from government say that caring forms part of the fabric and character of Britain.

- 1 in 8 people in Britain is now a carer – that is, 6.8 million people;
- 750,000 carers provide care for more than 50 hours a week;
- 75 per cent of people receiving care from carers living in the same household had no regular visits from professionals such as doctor, district nurse or social worker.

(*Source:* 'Facts about Carers' July 2002, Carers UK)

Helping you as carers is one of the best ways of helping the people you are caring for.

How this book can help you

Becoming a carer can change every aspect of your life, your relationships in the family and with others outside, and the way you live your life. It is up to you to decide how much or how little you want to take on and how much change you accept. This book can help you make those decisions. We outline some of the options open to you and the factors you might want to take into account.

There is lots of practical information about dealing with the everyday business of caring at home, from medication to moving and handling someone without damaging your back. We look at how the health and social care systems are organised and who to go to for particular kinds of help. We consider crises or difficult situations when you have to assess what is happening and make decisions about what to do. Throughout we provide pointers towards welfare benefit entitlements for carers but there is a whole chapter on legal and financial considerations related to caring. Beyond the crises come those difficult decisions about longer term care and we consider all the options there. If you are not sure what to look for in a care home, you can use our checklist of questions to ask.

When the person you are caring for dies, there are many things to do but you may find it difficult to think. Our last chapter will help you through that time and forward into your new life.

Your own needs as a carer are vitally important, so we have a whole chapter on how to identify your needs and meet them in a way that helps you to continue your important role for as long as you want or need to.

1 The caring role

In this chapter we look at what it means to be a carer. First we examine the wider picture of the situation for carers in general in the UK. Then we take an overview of what it means for individuals managing to care from day to day. Our focus is mainly, but not exclusively, on older people either as carers or as people being cared for. The topics covered include:

- Who carers are and who is being cared for
- Recognising yourself as a carer
- Definitions of disability
- You and the rest of your family
- You and your employment
- What can the social services department do to help you in your home?
- Having a break
- Domiciliary care
- Day centres and organised activities
- Respite care away from your own home
- Finding the services you need
- Giving something back

Who carers are and who is being cared for

Carers UK says that:

'A carer is someone looking after a friend, relative or neighbour who cannot manage without help because of sickness, age or disability.'

Carers are ordinary people, often carrying extraordinary responsibilities. They are of every age, culture, class and religion. The 2000 General Household Survey (GHS) suggests that more women than men are carers: 3.9 million compared with 2.9 million. The peak age for becoming a carer is between 45 and 64, and most commonly they are caring for parents. The GHS does not include information about young carers but research by Carers UK suggests that there may be as many as 51,000 carers under 16 in Great Britain (see Carers UK's Factsheet *Children and Young People who have Caring Responsibilities*).

'Disabled', as defined in section 29 of the National Assistance Act 1948, means: 'persons who are blind, deaf or dumb (or who suffer from mental disorder of any description), and other persons who are substantially and permanently handicapped by illness, injury or congenital deformity or such other disabilities as may be prescribed by the Secretary of State'. Mental disorder is defined (in section 1(2) of the Mental Health Act 1983) as 'mental illness, arrested or incomplete development of mind, psychopathic disorder and any other disorder or disability of mind'.

Recognising yourself as a carer

You may never have thought of yourself as a carer until someone else put the label on you. Most people who are carers don't think of themselves in those terms at all and may not like being described in that way. You might have described yourself as husband or wife (or mother or sister or son), and take it for granted that you will look after him or her. But there are advantages to accepting the label, however much you might dislike it.

Being a carer means that you have rights as well as caring responsibilities. The Carers Act 1995 and the Carers and Disabled Children Act 2000 gave carers in England and Wales legal rights. Statutory agencies such as the local authority's social services and the local office of the Department for Work and Pensions now recognise that, as a carer, you are entitled to:

■ welfare benefits;
■ assessment of your needs as a carer.

There are also many different voluntary agencies providing services that can support you in your role. But:

■ three-fifths of carers receive no regular visitor support services at all;
■ carers' needs are currently being met only patchily.

Case study

Sarah said:

'After my dad had been in hospital about two months, they decided to let him go home with what they called extreme aftercare as he had tubes everywhere. At first the district nurse visited him three times a day and the GP twice a week … they were both very good. Then they showed me how to change his dressings and everything, which felt very strange … you sort of change from daughter to parent. The visits from the district nurse gradually decreased until I was doing all the feeding, changing and washing … everything. Just by chance I'd been on a first aid course a few weeks before, so I was fairly familiar with lots of the jargon and knew about infection control and all that.

'We didn't have much to do with social services when Dad came out of hospital. I think it's because he was in hospital in London instead of locally. They found out that the nurses were coming in and decided that they didn't need to assess him. So I didn't have care assistants coming in to help get him up in the morning or put him back to bed at night – which I could have done with really. But the GP has been very good and arranged for Dad to go to a day centre now he's back on his feet …

because he was bored here, especially when I went back to work part-time. He potters about in the garden now and goes off to meet his friends at the day centre twice a week and goes on all the trips out. He pays for it all out of his pension and sorts out his own chiropody and hearing aid and everything himself.

'I'm only in my thirties but I had to give up full-time work. Now that everything's settled down I've been able to go back to work part-time but I've taken a big drop in income. But something like this happening to you sorts out your priorities – you decide what's really important in life.'

As Sarah said, becoming a carer can change every aspect of your life, your relationships in the family and with others outside and the way you live your life. Sarah agreed to take on a very full caring role for her father, which included giving up paid work. It is up to you to decide how much or how little you want to take on and how much change you accept.

What does it mean to be a carer?

Caring is a nice word but it's tough work emotionally, physically and financially. Your life will probably be restricted by the demands of caring for someone who cannot manage on their own for whatever reason – physical or mental health or disability. Some carers spend only a few hours a day or week caring, perhaps popping in regularly to make sure everything is all right. But it is easy for this low level support to gradually increase if the person you are caring for becomes less able to cope. In severe cases, caring can become a 24 hour a day, seven day a week job and it may go on for many years. Caring for a relative or partner can mean cutting back on food, giving up paid work and having no social life.

Caring will almost certainly affect your family relationships, with the person being cared for and with others in the family too. It can be emotionally draining. Carers' organisations where you meet other carers can help a lot when you are trying to come to terms with the role.

Case study

Penny, who is a member of a Rethink, told us:

'When our daughter Paula was admitted to mental hospital for the first time, Malcolm and I were just reeling with shock ... didn't know which way to turn ... and searching round for something ... or someone ... to grasp hold of ... some-one who knew what we were going through and might understand what was happening. Someone told me there was this group for people in our position and so I went to see the lady who ran it ... she lived near us so I just knocked on the door ... and it was such a relief to find someone to talk to. In the beginning you don't know what the diagnosis means or understand anything about the treat-ment. It's all new and frightening and you just don't know what to do. We were so anxious and fearful that it was almost a relief to be told she had schizophrenia. Then the guilt set in ... you ask yourself: what did we do wrong – we must have made a mistake somewhere – it must be our fault this has happened.

'But then there was the grief ... it's like losing the person without them dying. We lost the daughter we knew and it changed all our lives forever. At that stage we didn't know whether this was something that was just a one-off ... we had no idea it would go on and on for the rest of our lives ... perhaps it's just as well we couldn't see into the future.

'Paula was so creative and intelligent and had such potential. She will probably never do the ordinary things that other people's daughters do – get married, have children, have a career. She was a wonderful dancer and when she was young we thought she would do that for a living. We know now that she won't and that was hard to accept.

'But 15 years down the line we are much more together in ourselves. We see success in quite different terms ... like recently she was persuaded to go to the gym to an organised session and enjoyed it so much that she joined up of her own volition. She had to go by herself and relate to people there and that felt like a huge achievement.

'There's no doubt that Paula's health affects the relationship between us very deeply. She has her own flat these days so we are not in each other's pockets.

But when I see her I find I'm looking out for those little signs that will tell me something is going wrong ... those body language clues that she is going down hill. It's obvious she is going to pick up my anxiety ... it would be hard to ignore it, however much I try to lighten the atmosphere. It's difficult to relax ... and that tension goes on all the time, even when she isn't there. The anxiety affects everyone in the family and how we are with each other. I found it very difficult to concentrate at work as well and ended up taking early retirement just to relieve the pressure a bit. We find it really hard to go away on holiday because we just worry that she will go into crisis when we're not there. We are literally on call 24 hours a day every day, even though we don't live in the same house ... tense and waiting for the phone to ring – that's being a carer.'

As you can see from this example, every aspect of Penny and Malcolm's life has been affected by their daughter's illness, even though she doesn't live with them. In Chapter 7 we look at some of the strategies that carers can use to care for themselves, and in the 'Useful addresses' section there is a list of other agencies, including voluntary carers' organisations, that can help.

Irene's case is different because they all live in the same house.

Case study

Irene said:

'There's just me and my mum and my daughter. My mum looked after my dad until he died and by then she was so exhausted she couldn't cope on her own. So she moved in with us. To be honest, I thought she was so ill she wouldn't last long but with a bit of TLC she soon recovered. That was ten years ago and now I think she'll live forever. She'd much rather be living on her own but she was so far away from us that it wasn't practical. At the time it seemed to make sense that, if she was going to move, she might as well come here.

'She was in a big sprawling bungalow before – all on one floor with plenty of space for all that huge old furniture and all her knick-knacks. She hates our house, which she says is pokey and inconvenient. We've got stairs and the kitchen is too small for more than one person at a time. I like my old-fashioned seventies stuff because I've got used to it over the years but my daughter likes the modern, light wood stuff, so we already had a bit of a mixture when Mum brought all her stuff and we've turned into a junk shop … you can hardly move. Her stuff was too big really but she likes it, so what could I do?

'Well, we've always been close … but I don't mean lovey-dovey. We argue a lot … and sometimes I'm afraid to go out in case there's blood on the walls when I come back. I think my daughter can't wait to get her own place. She's 25 now but everywhere's so expensive she can't afford to go. Anyway we're okay … we'll manage.

'Mum says: "I look at it like this. Why should I pay £400 a week to be miserable in a nursing home when I can be miserable here for nothing?"'

Irene is one of what some people call the 'sandwich generation': caught in the middle with parent(s) and children making demands on her at the same time. Families come in many different shapes and sizes. Relatives may live close to one another or they may be separated by miles or even by oceans. They may spend a lot of time in each other's company or speak on the phone regularly. On the other hand, they may not speak to each other or meet from one year's end to the next.

Carers provide most of the care in the community. If you are still working, it is difficult to be a carer and hold down a paid job at the same time. This can restrict your ability to earn a living or save for a pension. In turn, that means you are much more likely to become dependent on welfare benefits when you get older yourself, and this is a serious consideration. It is something you should take into account if you are faced with a choice about what to do. Over all, it is estimated that carers provide support to others worth £57 billion a year (data from Carers UK 2002).

Caring is an issue that potentially affects all of us – we are all likely to be carers or to be cared for at some time in our lives. Childcare is relatively predictable – it can be planned for and usually lasts for a definite period of time. Other caring responsibilities can happen overnight, so they often can't be planned for and can last indefinitely. In Penny and Malcolm's situation they eventually became older carers looking after a younger relative. Parents naturally expect their children to eventually become independent, both emotionally and financially, and expect them to want to leave home.

Case study

Penny said:

'Paula lived with us for a long time but eventually we decided she had to leave home. We started to worry about how she would survive if anything happened to us – she needed to be independent. As long as we were happy to have her here the professionals didn't raise the subject. But her care co-ordinator was very helpful when we said we could no longer have her living with us. She helped us to put her name down on the council housing list. She had quite a lot of points because of her mental health problems but we still had to wait about a year before she was allocated a flat. At the time it felt like a really hard decision but it was the best thing for her in the long run.

'Once she moved out, she got far more services than she had before – I think her quality of life improved enormously. She has a community mental health nurse visiting once a week to make sure she is taking her medication, and a community care worker goes twice a week to take her shopping and get her involved in all sorts of activities … art group, cooking … that sort of thing. It was the right decision but it took us a long time to take it and then a lot of determination to make it happen.'

Penny, Malcolm and Paula had some tough decisions to make and, as Penny said, one of those decisions was about giving up work. This is the area we consider next.

What are your options if you are thinking of leaving work?

If you are of working age and thinking about leaving work, you need to consider whether you want to and, if not, what alternative there could be. First, think about the things you will be giving up and whether you really want to lose them.

- Will you manage with less money?
- Do you want to give up the independence and social contact you have through work?
- Will you lose valuable skills if you leave work?
- Can you afford to lose your occupational pension?

Then think about ways around the problem. Could you:

- Work part-time or share your job?
- Do some or all of your work from home?
- Take paid or unpaid leave for a period while you think about the longer term?
- Get help from your local office of the Department for Work and Pensions, the local authority social services department (in Scotland, the social work department; in Northern Ireland, the department for social development) or the local health service?
- Arrange for someone else to help by taking on some of your caring responsibilities?

Remember that employers value skilled, experienced and committed members of staff and are keen to retain them. Your employer may be able to help in ways you had not thought possible. Talk to them about your situation, directly or through your personnel officer, union representative or staff association. Under the European Union's Part Time Workers Directive, part-time workers have more rights than they used to, so it is worthwhile finding out about these, too, if you are considering going part-time. Carers UK is working with carers' organisations and major employers to come up with solutions to the problems that carers experience in the workplace.

If you ask for help from your local social services department, social work department or department for social development, remember that they are required to assess your needs as well as those of the person you care for. If you want to work, they must take this into account when they assess what services they can offer. They may be able to:

- Provide direct support (eg a 'home help' or a day centre place)
- Help you get financial support from the Independent Living Fund
- Tell you about private care facilities that are registered and approved
- Tell you about organisations or local support groups that can help
- Give information about welfare benefits available

Making alternative care arrangements so that you can work may be the best option but it can also create conflict or cause feelings of guilt. What you decide must be right for you as well as for others. You have the right to choose and that means choosing whether to give up work or to continue to earn an income. If you decide to leave work, think about options other than resigning:

- Take a career break
- Opt for voluntary redundancy
- Take early retirement

Talk to your personnel officer, union representative or staff association about what is possible. Contact Carers UK for help with benefit entitlements (contact details on page 262). Action for Carers and Employment is a national project aiming to address the barriers faced by carers who wish to work.

What if I want to return to work?

If you gave up work to become a carer and now want to return, this affects your benefit entitlement. You lose your entitlement to Carers Allowance as soon as you stop being a carer. If you receive Carer Premium, this continues for a further period, after which you will be expected to register for work at the local JobCentre unless you are sick.

Registering for work protects your National Insurance record (including state pension contributions). You will also be able to find out if you are eligible for Jobseeker's Allowance and schemes such as New Deal or New Deal 50 Plus.

Employers who take on former carers can sometimes benefit from paying less National Insurance for a period. The local office of the Department for Work and Pensions will tell you more about these schemes. You may be entitled to the same level of Housing Benefit and Council Tax Benefit (Rate Rebate in Northern Ireland) for a few weeks after you return to work. This will help you manage until your first salary is paid.

Whether you are a former carer or still caring, you may need support in returning to work after a period out of the workplace. Many colleges and adult education centres run courses for people returning to work. Most will include:

- Confidence building
- Time or stress management
- Identifying skills
- Identifying training needs
- Job search skills

These courses will not necessarily be specific to carers. Many training providers can make reductions to fees for carers who are receiving state benefits.

Juggling care and work

Four million people in the UK juggle work and care, and nearly three million of these carers look after an older relative. Our ageing population means more and more of us will end up caring for an older relative – and many of tomorrow's parents will also have 'elder care' responsibilities. *Carers UK*

If you are a working carer, you are probably trying to deal with the stresses of doing two jobs – one paid and one unpaid.

> ## Case study
>
> **Jen** works in a call centre and cares for her mother.
>
> 'The most difficult thing about working and caring for my mother is that it's like having two jobs instead of one. It's a case of having to juggle things so I can look after my mother and come to work … managing to do everything in a day that needs to be done.'

Carers face a range of problems in the world of work. Inflexible employers, unsympathetic colleagues and JobCentre staff who lack awareness mean that many carers find it hard to get or hold down a job. Former carers also find the job market difficult to return to, as they may have gaps in their knowledge or CVs (curriculum vitae – your record of education and employment) owing to caring.

As a working carer you may feel unable to share your caring experiences at work because you feel that you will be viewed as less able to do your paid job. But two-thirds of working-age carers are in paid employment. With the right support, you can do both. Flexibility is of central importance and sometimes this can be negotiated.

Should I tell my employer?

The question of whether to tell your employer is a difficult one. You can find out whether your employer has a policy to support carers by asking the right person at work; for example:

- personnel officer;
- welfare officer or occupational health adviser;
- union or staff association representative;
- colleagues.

There are usually several people who might have the information you need, so you don't have to talk first to your line manager if you don't want to. There may be existing support that you are unaware of. On the other hand, you may find that your employer is open to exploring ways to support carers. Colleagues may be more supportive than you think. It may help simply to discuss your situation with someone you can trust at work. You might find that some colleagues are also carers. Together you may be able to talk to your employer about ways in which you could be supported.

Barclays Bank has more than 84,000 employees in the UK and provides a good example of what employers can do. When it carried out a survey, it found out that more than half of its staff had caring responsibilities. Carers wanted more flexibility in working time and better understanding of the problems they faced in trying to match their caring responsibilities with their work.

Carers UK says that carer-friendly employment policies make good sense for employers in terms of:

- cost – through reduced turnover of staff and less absenteeism;
- flexibility for employers – labour availability and matching of work;
- motivation of employees – resulting in improved morale;
- performance of the business over all.

Recent moves by the Government towards 'family friendly' employment provide for employees to ask for unpaid leave for family emergencies. The policy package for carers introduced in 2002 includes:

- new legislation to allow local authorities to address carers' needs;
- entitlement to a second pension for time spent caring;
- proposals for increased income;
- reductions in Council Tax for carers of disabled people;
- carers' centres;
- extending help to return to work;
- census question to collect information about carers;
- support for young carers, including help at school;
- funding for breaks for carers.

As a working carer, you are likely to need a range of support in the workplace. This will probably mean a different level of support at different

13

times – from access to a telephone to check on the person you care for, to leave arrangements that fit around hospital discharge. Carers UK has two booklets that you might find helpful – *Juggling Work and Care*, for carers who are in employment, and *Carers at Work*, aimed at employers to encourage carer-friendly work practices.

Case study

In **Jen's** case:

'The flexibility and support that my employer provides are crucial – the company has had a very sympathetic approach to me, which makes it a lot easier for me to be relaxed at work and concentrate on my job.

'If I need to call Mum during the day when I am worried about her, I have access to a telephone. I can go somewhere private to have a chat with her instead of worrying all day.

'The carers' policy has given me a lot of leeway. For example, I can arrange flexible starting and finishing times, which are set each week. If Mum is ill, I can call at short notice and ask for time off. I can have time off to take her to a hospital appointment or to be at home when she is discharged from hospital. If I need longer, I can take half the time as annual leave and the company matches it by giving me paid carer's leave for the rest. If things became really difficult, I could take a career break and my job would be open to me when I was able to return.'

Carers are now legally entitled to time off for emergencies under the Employment Relations Act (or Employment Relations (Northern Ireland) Order 1999 in Northern Ireland). This gives you:

- the right to take a 'reasonable' amount of time off work to deal with an emergency involving a dependant. This right also protects employees from victimisation or dismissal if they use it. It is up to employers whether leave is paid or unpaid;
- the right to parental leave, for children born on or after 15 December 1999, which can be taken up to a child's fifth birthday, or up to the eighteenth birthday for a disabled child.

Finding the services you need

If you need support in your caring role, you should first get in touch with your local authority social services department, or your family doctor (GP), to see if they can give you some advice or support.

Local authorities have a duty, under the National Health Service and Community Care Act 1990, to carry out a care assessment of people who appear to them to need community care services, which they may provide or arrange on your behalf. 'Care assessment' is a term used to describe how the social services department finds out about the sort of help and support you may need. Sometimes this is also called a needs assessment.

Every NHS Trust should have or be developing a Patient Advice and Liaison Service (PALS). PALS should provide support and information about local health services to patients, carers and families.

NHS Direct is a telephone advice and information service staffed by experienced nurses (contact details on page 249). It provides advice and information about health, illnesses and health services. NHS Direct is available throughout England. There is also a website that gives information about health services, treatment choices, medical conditions and self-help groups. In Scotland there is NHS24 (see page 249).

Your local Age Concern or carers' centre may be able to tell you about special services in your area, which they or other organisations run. There may be support groups, for example for people who have had a stroke or have mental health problems. They may also know of people seeking work for a few hours or days per week, perhaps to help out with the garden or heavier household tasks, or shopping. Local Age Concerns provide different services, but larger ones are likely to provide services such as day centres, advocacy, volunteer visitors, befriending or practical help. (See the 'Useful addresses' section for details of these and other organisations that can help.)

What can the social services department do to help you in your home?

Each local authority social services department offers different kinds of help and support, and has its own ways of deciding how much, if anything, you will have to pay. Some services may be provided direct by the social services department – these are often called 'in-house services'. Social services departments may also arrange for services to be provided on their behalf by another organisation, such as a charity or a private agency; they do this by making a contract with the organisation for the service. Another alternative that local authorities must now offer is a Direct Payment, whereby the local authority gives you funds to buy the care yourself instead of providing services itself.

Local authorities all have their own 'eligibility criteria', which they use to decide who qualifies for the help that they provide. They assess each person's needs against these eligibility criteria. If your needs meet the criteria, social services must provide help to meet those needs. Eligibility criteria vary among local authorities, but the framework outlined by the Department of Health – Fair Access to Care Services (FACS) – is intended to reduce these variations.

Services that help people to stay in their own homes, or support people in sheltered housing, are often collectively called domiciliary and day care; sometimes they are called non-residential services. They may also be called community care services. Below are some of the most common services.

- Equipment and adaptations – if you have difficulty in managing certain tasks, there may be gadgets or equipment available that can help you. For example, special taps for people who have difficulty using ordinary ones. 'Adaptations' are changes to your home to help you get about or manage better. (See Chapter 2 for further information.)
- Alarm systems.

16

- Day care.
- Home help, or home care assistant.
- Direct Payments – the Health and Social Care Act 2001 requires local authorities to give some people money to purchase their own care instead of (or as well as) providing or arranging the community care services. The Carers and Disabled Children Act 2000 enables Direct Payments to be made to carers.
- Laundry – some social services departments provide a laundry service for people with incontinence, or who cannot manage their laundry for other reasons.
- Meals at home – sometimes called 'meals on wheels'.
- Respite care – taking a break.
- Telephones – help with cost of installing an essential phone can come from social services or from a voluntary organisation; your phone company will advise on situations where there is difficulty in using the phone (eg because of a disability).
- Family doctor and community health services – district nurse or health visitor; chiropodist; continence adviser; physiotherapist; community mental health nurse; hospice at home or Macmillan nurse.
- Local voluntary organisations and support groups (eg Age Concern and carers' centres).
- Hospital after-care schemes – schemes, usually run by voluntary organisations, that can help people over the first few days or weeks after a stay in hospital.
- A companion at home – helping with light care tasks, or just 'keeping a watchful eye'.
- Employment or nursing agencies – private agencies that will recruit and place living-in companions who help with housework but not personal care. Those providing personal care, nurses and care workers will have to register with the General Social Care Council (GSCC) as domiciliary care agencies. The GSCC is also to hold a list of people considered unsuitable to work with vulnerable adults.
- Help with housing (see Chapter 6).
- Help with paying for care (see Chapters 4 and 6).
- Social security benefits (see Chapter 4).

Getting a break

However well organised you are, everyone needs a break. Your needs are as important as the needs of the person you care for (see Chapter 7 for more information on looking after yourself). It will benefit both of you when you return to the caring role refreshed and reinvigorated. It is sometimes difficult to remember that the person you are caring for may benefit from a break, too.

Respite means taking a break. Respite care could be for a few hours, one night or a day, or longer – for example, a week or two weeks. If you need a break, you can ask social services for a carer's assessment. When your needs have been assessed, it may be able to purchase services for you, or make Direct Payments (see Chapter 4 for John's story) or give vouchers so that you can purchase help for yourself.

Here we look at some of the options available to give both of you a bit of time off:

- domiciliary care and sitting services;
- day centres and organised activities;
- respite care away from home.

Domiciliary care and sitting services

Domiciliary care is care provided in your own home. Domiciliary care agencies have to register with the Commission for Social Care Inspection (CSCI). In the past, 'home helps' used to do a range of useful jobs about the house, including cleaning and other housework. In most local authority areas, social services departments no longer provide this kind of help. Funding for domiciliary care is now focused on personal care for those who need help with tasks such as bathing, toileting, getting up and dressed in the morning or getting into bed at night. If you want help with housework, you will probably have to pay for that and arrange it privately with one of the many agencies that advertise in your local press. If you know of other people in your position, it would be worthwhile asking them who they use and find out whether they do a good job at a reasonable price. Personal recommendation is a good guide.

Sitting services can let you take a few hours off in the day time or get a good night's undisturbed sleep. The largest scheme of this kind is run by a voluntary organisation called Crossroads – Caring for Carers (contact details on page 237). Crossroads was set up with the aim of providing short-term breaks to carers in their own homes.

Information about voluntary organisations that offer this service can be found through the telephone directory, local libraries, local Age Concerns or local carers' projects such as the centres linked to The Princess Royal Trust for Carers or the Council for Voluntary Service (CVS) (contact details on pages 250 and 248).

Day centres and organised activities

Social contact is very important for everyone – both carers and those who are cared for. Many people belong to community organisations and clubs as a way of meeting others and keeping themselves active. If you take on the caring role for someone, it will benefit both of you if you can manage to keep up those contacts. Sometimes friends will provide transport and substitute care for a couple of hours. Or, depending on the circumstances, you may need to pay a carer to take on that role.

Local colleges and adult education centres offer regular classes in a wide range of subjects to suit every taste, from art and crafts through languages, computing and cookery to exercise and philosophy. If the person you care for needs assistance while they are away from you, talk to the college to see if it has any arrangements to fit these circumstances. Alternatively, you might want to make your own arrangements with a volunteer or paid helper.

Many groups and associations run lunch clubs, drop-in centres and social activities that can provide a break for carers. Day centres may be run by social services or by voluntary organisations such as Age Concern or MIND (contact details on page 247). They can offer a wide range of services such as:

- social activities (eg board games);
- educational classes (eg art and crafts);
- outings (eg to stately homes and gardens or the theatre);
- work-related opportunities where relevant (eg gardening, office studies, making items for sale, or food preparation);
- counselling;
- alternative therapies (eg aromatherapy, reflexology);
- meals and coffee mornings and drop-in café;
- bathing for those who need assistance;
- domiciliary care that goes out to people at home.

Attending a day centre provides a change of scene and occupation for the person being cared for as well as respite for you, the carer.

Respite care away from home

Respite care away from home can be provided in care homes by:

- the NHS – for nursing care needs;
- the social services department – for non-nursing care needs.

For most people, it will be the local authority that provides respite care, and you may be asked to pay towards it. This care is usually provided in a care home, which may be run by a private or voluntary organisation or by the local authority itself. The payment arrangements depend on the income and 'capital assets' of the person who is being cared for (see Chapter 6 for more information on charges for residential care).

If someone has continuing nursing care needs, the NHS must arrange and fund an adequate level of respite health care. This applies particularly to people who:

- have intensive or complex health care needs and require specialist medical or nursing supervision or assessment during a period of respite care;
- could benefit from active rehabilitation during a period of respite care;
- have a terminal illness and are receiving palliative care for their symptoms (eg pain control) in their own homes but where they or their carer need a period of respite care.

Local NHS bodies must have agreements with local authorities over who provides respite care under which circumstances. In most cases the costs are split between NHS and local authority, and reflect the level of nursing care required. With purely residential care, you may have to contribute towards the local authority element of the payment. The NHS contribution is not means-tested but the amount paid depends on a nurse assessing the level of care required (see Chapter 6 for more information). If the person's stay is planned to last less than six weeks, they will not necessarily receive a detailed assessment. They should be assigned to an appropriate 'band' based on information that is available from medical records.

In conclusion, respite is an important aspect of caring. It can make the difference between you as carer feeling able to cope and remaining in reasonable health or, on the other hand, becoming so exhausted that you have to stop or become ill yourself.

Giving something back

Research produced by Carers UK shows that people who care for sick or disabled relatives are also putting long hours into voluntary and community work, increasingly acting as drivers of social change. Carers of all ages, backgrounds and situations are involved in local community work, putting in an average of 18 hours a month – with nearly one in ten contributing over 30 hours a month, on top of their caring responsibilities.

Over half the carers who responded to a survey by Carers UK in 2002 (*Adding Value: carers as drivers of social change*) were actively involved in voluntary activities such as:

- setting up and running local self-help groups;
- sitting on NHS or local authority advisory bodies;
- raising money for charities;
- campaigning for local amenities;
- helping with day-care services for disabled adults or children.

Carers' involvement in health and social care development and delivery should ensure that local services take carers' needs into account. Carers are also likely to gain and update key skills through their involvement in supporting other carers, which may help them return to paid work.

In a Time Bank scheme, participants earn credits for helping each other – an hour of your time entitles you to an hour of someone else's. Credits are deposited centrally in the Time Bank and 'withdrawn' when you need help yourself. Time credits have no monetary value, so they are unlikely to affect carers' benefits.

Most people do not actively choose to become carers – it is something life thrusts upon them. And for many carers, the day-to-day trials of looking after someone can be a gruelling experience. Carers UK says that its study found that thousands of carers are able to turn the frustrations of dealing with red tape and their empathy with people in a similar position into an asset that can benefit their local community. Many of the best voluntary and self-help projects grow out of local communities taking action to help themselves. Increasingly, carers are becoming community activists – helping out at grass-roots level, advising or cajoling decision-makers and campaigning for social change. This can only be a positive development, both for carers and for their communities.

Case study

As **Gillian**, a carer, put it:

'Only by having the experience of being a carer do you truly understand the demands, both physically and emotionally, that it has on your own well-being. I don't believe I went through all of this not to do something with all it taught me. Speaking out on behalf of carers is now my full-time commitment. I know what I am talking about because I have been there.'

Key points

- Carers are ordinary people, often carrying extraordinary responsibilities.

- Caring is an issue that potentially affects all of us – we are all likely to be carers or to be cared for at some time in our lives.

- One person in eight in Britain is now a carer – 6.8 million people.

- 750,000 carers provide care for more than 50 hours a week.

- Most people who are carers don't think of themselves in those terms at all and may not like being described in that way.

- It is difficult to be a carer and hold down a paid job at the same time. This can restrict your ability to earn a living, and you become dependent on welfare benefits when you get older yourself.

- Two-thirds of working-age carers are in paid employment. With the right support, you can do both.

- If you are of working age and thinking of leaving work, you need to consider whether you want to, and, if not, what alternatives there could be: take a career break; opt for voluntary redundancy; take early retirement.

- If you want to return to work, many colleges and adult education centres run courses to help people in your position.

- As a carer you have rights as well as caring responsibilities.

- You are entitled to welfare benefits and assessment of your needs as a carer.

- The local authority social services department will assess your needs as well as those of the person you care for, and can provide a range of day and domiciliary care and respite services to support you both.

- Direct Payments offer you the opportunity to purchase these care services for yourself.

2 Daily essentials

In this chapter we look at some of the essential elements of daily living, such as:

- medication
- nutrition
- encouraging exercise
- moving and handling someone
- practical equipment
- coping with difficult conditions
- making your home a safer environment
- use of keys and locks

Carers find a variety of ways of dealing with the everyday business of living and caring.

Case study

Ian's mother May has physical disabilities that make it difficult for her to walk much, and she is always worried about falling. **Ian** said:

'Mum can get herself out of bed and get her own clothes on but she likes to have a shower every morning and I need to be there to help her with that. We used to use a bath but getting in and out of that was really difficult. She slipped once and I couldn't lift her up, so we had the bath taken out and a shower put in instead.

Drinking tea and having a chat.
Photographs by Helen Stone. Reproduced by courtesy of Carers UK

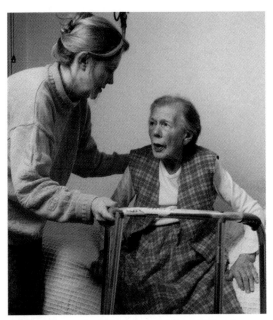

Helping her mother-in-law with her walking frame.

Feeding her grandmother some yoghurt.
Photographs by Geoff Wilson. Reproduced by courtesy of Carers UK

Helping her husband to put on his socks and shoes.

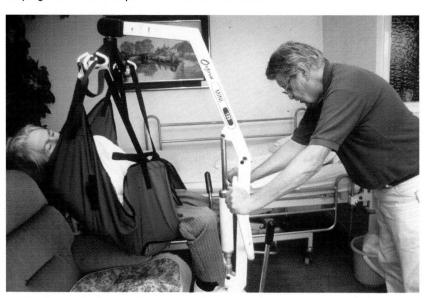

Husband and wife demonstrating how to use a hoist.
Photographs by Sam Tanner. Reproduced by courtesy of Carers UK

She can manage to get down the stairs provided she takes them slowly, and it's good exercise.'

Ian is a local councillor so he has to plan ahead to make arrangements for when he has meetings to go to.

'I do the housework as she can't manage that at all really, but we do the shopping together, and if I leave Mum the ingredients for meals she can manage the cooking. She can't bend down to use the oven but she can use the microwave because it is at the right height. If I'm out for part of the day she will watch television quite happily. So she chooses what she wants to watch and I programme it for her. I think it's very important to keep up the social contacts and there are lots of things she can go to in the afternoons: flower arranging, art classes, and the ladies' tea group. One of her friends often picks her up to go to those. I take her to antique fairs or out to lunch sometimes, too. It all depends on what else I've got on that week but I think keeping up her social contacts is vital for both of us. She puts herself to bed if I'm out in the evening, so that's a help.'

As you can see from this example, Ian organises his life with his mother's needs in mind. The house has been slightly adapted for her and he has to work out a daily routine that keeps her occupied and happy while he is busy with other things.

Medication

It is likely that the person you are caring for will be taking prescribed medicines of some kind, depending on their state of health. Your role may include one or more of the following:

- simply understanding what is being taken and why;
- ensuring safe storage at an appropriate temperature;
- making sure medicines are available to be taken regularly;
- thinking and planning ahead about repeat prescriptions.

The best place to start is probably to make sure that the person you are caring for knows what they are taking and why. However, it is important not to take over the doctor's role.

You can probably help by making sure the doctor or nurse who does the prescribing explains everything fully. If you are not sure what the medication is, you can read about it in the instructions that come with the packaging. This will also tell you about any side-effects that you might want to look out for. If you are worried about side-effects, always ask for further advice.

Case study

Tom said:

'I had to step in once when the doctor changed my wife's medication and she started behaving really oddly. I was so worried that I phoned my son and got him to come over and see what was happening. We really started to panic because we thought Christine was showing signs of dementia. Fortunately, we have a good relationship with our GP – I can always talk to him on the phone if I'm worried about anything, and he will see us the same day if he can. I told him what was happening and the upshot of it was that Christine was rushed into hospital to be 'detoxed' from the side-effects of this medication. It's a good thing I was there because I don't know that anyone else would have realised what was happening.'

If either of you has any questions about a drug, the pharmacist should be able to answer them.

There are three kinds of drugs licensed for use in the UK by the Medicines Control Agency:

- *Prescription-only* medicines, prescribed by a doctor, dentist or prescribing nurse, and supplied by a pharmacist.
- *Pharmacy* medicines, or 'over-the-counter' medicines, which can be bought without a prescription but only in a pharmacist/chemist shop (eg stronger pain-killers).

- *General sales list* (GSL) drugs, which can be bought in many different places such as supermarkets (eg ordinary pain-killers and laxatives).

Prescribed drugs always come with instructions on how often and how many to take, whether with meals or at particular times of the day. It is important for the person you care for to follow the instructions but also to remain as far as possible in control of their own medication regimen. It is all too easy for a carer to slip into the habit of providing pills at the appropriate time and for the person who is being cared for to give up bothering to remember. This type of 'institutionalisation' can happen as easily at home as it can anywhere else.

Patient power is important, and prescribed medicines belong to the person whose name is printed on the label. Except in special circumstances under the Mental Health Act 1983, everyone has the right to refuse treatment. As carer, you will probably become anxious if the person you are caring for refuses to take their medication. If that happens, your best course of action is to talk to the pharmacist or nurse or GP about your anxieties. Otherwise, you may find yourself in a position where your relationship becomes damaged through getting into an ongoing battle.

Do encourage the person you are caring for to be honest with the doctor or nurse who is prescribing for them. Sometimes people stop taking medicines because they don't like the side-effects or they are difficult to swallow, and then feel anxious about telling the doctor. It is important that the doctor has a true picture of what is happening if they are going to be able to treat the condition. The doctor may otherwise be puzzled if symptoms persist when the medication prescribed should have solved the problem. They may be able to change the prescription to another preparation that would be tolerated better.

Just because over-the-counter drugs are freely available does not mean they are harmless. They may alter the effectiveness of other, prescribed, medicines and may also have unwanted effects, so they should be used with caution. Ask the pharmacist for advice if either of you is not sure what to do.

Many people find complementary therapies such as acupuncture, homoeopathy or herbal remedies useful. The relationship between complementary therapies and the NHS has changed over time and nowadays some GPs will suggest going to an osteopath, for example, or recommend yoga as a good way to keep supple. However, it is always wise to make sure you know as much as possible about the practitioner you want to go to, for example their qualifications. You might perhaps look for personal recommendation from a satisfied customer, because you will normally have to pay for this kind of treatment.

You also need to know that there may be unwanted side-effects from complementary therapies just as there are from conventional ones. There have been instances where a herbal remedy has caused serious illness and even, rarely, death. Be sure to tell your GP about any such therapies you decide to use, because they may have an effect on the medicine he or she prescribes. For example, St John's wort, which some people take if they are feeling depressed, should not be taken during pregnancy.

Nutrition

Food has a special place in our lives that goes far beyond its nutritional function. Particular foods may remind us of past events and experiences: of picnics in the park and parties or school dinners or wartime. It can be a symbol of love, have a spiritual significance or represent a sense of belonging to a particular family or community. When we are feeling unwell or vulnerable, those associations become particularly important. Familiar food brings comfort and reassurance that, in some respects at least, the world has not changed.

Healthy eating

Healthy eating is important for all of us but there are particular conditions such as diabetes or heart disease where diet has a key role to play. A healthy diet is only part of being healthy, of course: being the right weight and getting enough exercise are vital too. The current nutritional guidelines for healthy adults include:

- reduce the total amount of fat, but especially saturated fat;
- reduce sugar intake;
- increase dietary fibre;
- reduce salt intake;
- eat five portions of fruit and/or vegetables a day;
- drink plenty of fluid (eg at least 8 cups a day – not alcoholic!).

From childhood, meals may be a time when people exert their individuality by refusing certain foods, expressing likes and dislikes. They can be a time of confrontation when refusal of food is seen by the cook as a sign of rejection. The table can become a place where family relationships are played out, where people express their feelings about themselves and each other and their lives together. This can make your role as carer a difficult balancing act, particularly if you try to take responsibility for making sure someone else eats well. You can play your part by listening to the dietary advice given by the experts and adapting meals as required.

Food selection and choice

Many factors affect the food choices we make:

- Availability of food (eg range stocked in local shops; who does the shopping).
- Access (eg distance between home and shops, and mobility or cost of travel).
- Income or budgeting skills and cost of food.
- Cooking facilities.
- Cooking and food preparation knowledge, skills and abilities.
- Cooking for self and/or others.
- Cultural traditions and religious beliefs.
- Habit and previous experiences of food.
- Likes and dislikes.
- Knowledge about diet and nutrition.

- State of health (eg affecting appetite).
- Willingness to experiment.

If a change of diet is necessary, it usually has to be made gradually – you can't change the habits of a lifetime overnight. If you try to make someone eat things they don't like, the chances are they will simply 'dig their heels in'. When it comes to the crunch, the person you are providing food for has to take responsibility for themselves. The alternative could mean confrontation and cheating, psychological game-playing and misery for everyone.

If you want advice on feeding someone with a specific condition such as diabetes, have a look at Age Concern's *Carer's Handbook* series or, for more general advice, *Nutritional Care for Older People* from its care professional handbook series.

Encouraging simple exercise

Regular simple exercise in the context of healthy eating and living can help to maintain our ability to function. Research into ageing and exercise has shown that exercise can increase the stamina of an older person and increase the capacity for independent living by as much as 10–20 years. People who exercise regularly are more likely to maintain bone and muscle mass, stamina, power and suppleness. It also increases appetite and helps to avoid day-to-day problems such as leg ulcers and constipation. Exercising with others in a group promotes conversation and is an opportunity to socialise but even exercising alone has benefits in terms of increasing a sense of well-being. Exercise increases social confidence and benefits mood and self-esteem as well as making it easier to carry out the daily tasks of living.

As a carer you can encourage simple exercise using a reference book such as Age Concern's *Alive and Kicking*. It gives advice on:

- fitness for older people;
- health and safety when exercising;

- structuring exercise sessions;
- including activity in existing daily routines;
- sample exercise plans;
- promoting good mental health – stress, relaxation and breathing;
- exercise, older people and health improvement.

Many of the exercises outlined in the book are carried out while sitting in an upright chair. There is also lots of advice on tailoring the exercises to the fitness of each person and making sure they are appropriate and safe.

Fitness means different things to different people. What does it mean to you? Maybe you thought of:

- Being able to go up and down stairs without getting out of breath.
- Being able to do what you want to do and still have some energy left at the end of the day.
- Being able to get dressed without assistance.

For some older people, fitness will mean being able to continue playing a sport even if perhaps a less vigorous sport than in the past, for example bowling. The British Heart Foundation recommends that everyone walks 5 kilometres a day to keep a healthy heart. But this may not be a realistic aim for someone with a physical disability.

Case study

Ivy is 85 and has arthritis and osteoporosis but she still goes bowling two or three times a week. She enjoys the companionship and social side but still plays to win.

'When we play in a tournament, the other team have often heard of me. I've heard people say: "Oh no, Ivy's not playing is she? We might as well go home now!" That makes me laugh. If I stop winning I won't want to play any more. I wouldn't want to let the side down.'

Most of us are fortunate enough to have the choice to exercise or not, and there is a variety of activities, clubs, organisations, equipment and suitably trained people to meet our needs. Walking, for example, is a popular activity for older people, and Ramblers Clubs flourish all over the UK. The Ramblers' Association is Britain's biggest walking organisation with over 136,000 members across England, Scotland and Wales and hundreds of affiliated groups (for contact details, see page 251).

Case study

Ethel walks with her local Ramblers Club nearly every week:

'I arrange for someone to come in and look after my sister while I have the day off to go walking. I suppose it's quite a big club because we are able to find leaders not just for the traditional Sunday walks but we also go out on Wednesdays. Mid-week there is a choice of walks, too. Often I can choose whether to do a whole day's ten mile walk, or half a day. The different groups also walk at different speeds. We have quite a wide range of ages and abilities among the members – Harry is 90 and still able to do ten miles. If I'm not feeling up to the mark I go on the short leisurely walk, where we usually end up with a pub lunch. It's a good social meeting point and the exercise does me the world of good. My mind sort of goes into 'overdrive' when I get into the rhythm of walking – it calms me down and worries just float away.'

Many older people, however, find their choice of activity more and more restricted and tend to lose mobility gradually. When this happens, simple exercises carried out in the comfort of your own home help a lot, and this is where carers can come in.

The chair exercises detailed in *Alive and Kicking* are useful for most older people, from those who are completely independent and mobile to those who have limited mobility and require a range of support from carers. The exercises include movements for:

- shoulders
- chest
- head and neck
- back
- face
- wrists, hands and fingers
- legs and hip
- ankles, feet and toes.

There are also exercises to do standing up if you want to and some to do lying down on a bed, too.

Case study

Ethel said:

'I do some stretching exercises every morning while I'm still lying down. It helps to get my muscles and joints moving before I actually have to put a foot to the floor. Sometimes the twinges are quite painful when I first start and I think it would be so much easier not to bother. But on days when I've been in too much of a hurry to get somewhere and missed out the exercises, I always regret it. I think it helps me to stand properly, with my back straight instead of stooped. It tones up the muscles and protects my back when I'm looking after my sister (see 'Moving and handling people', overleaf).'

There are different levels of exercise:

- Warm-up exercises to wake the body up.
- Endurance activities to make the heart and lungs work harder.
- Strengthening exercises for the muscles and joints, some using elasticated resistance bands.
- Stretching and cooling-down exercises to tone and lengthen the muscles around the joints.
- Relaxation with deep breathing to reduce the negative effects of stress and tension.

It is recommended that you work out a weekly exercise plan and try to stick to it. This could just mean a couple of exercises once or twice a day or 10-minute sessions perhaps four times a week. Your role as carer in this is perhaps to initiate exercise and then to join in, perhaps demonstrating new exercises and providing support and encouragement. They will certainly do you good, too, and help to protect your back.

Moving and handling people

Many carers provide personal help with toileting and bathing, including physically demanding tasks involving moving people from one place to another. We can only give you general advice here on how to protect yourself, as carer, from hurting yourself while looking after someone else. The best advice is specific to your situation and comes from an expert who can properly assess the risks that you are exposed to. In the meantime, while you are waiting for a full professional assessment, here are some general pointers. For more information, try reading *Safer Handling of People in the Community* produced by BackCare and available for purchase from its website (contact details on page 230). It is written for paid care workers but has lots of useful advice in it.

As carer, your health and safety are vital. Unlike paid carers, you don't have an employer who could be held responsible if you hurt yourself. Your health and safety are your own responsibility.

Do not lift a person (or a heavy object) if you can possibly find any other way of moving them from one place or position to another.

- Decide what it is you want to do – where the person is now and where you want to move them to – and assess the situation.
- Make sure the space is clear of obstructions (eg furniture or small objects on the floor).
- Find and put into position any equipment or aids that will help to reduce the strain on you (eg if you are fortunate enough to have a hoist, use it whenever possible).

- Know yourself and your capabilities – be clear about what you can and can't do.
- Talk to the person you are going to move: explain what you are proposing to do and what you want them to do – maybe they can help by taking some of their own weight on their arms.
- Get yourself into the right position:
  - put your feet apart with your leading foot forward to provide stability (see Figure 1);
  - make sure your spine has its natural curves and is protected by firm muscles round it – don't twist;
  - stand as close as possible to the person you are moving, get a good hold and keep your shoulders relaxed and elbows in;
  - bend your knees and hips so that the strong muscles of your legs and buttocks can take the strain.
- Try to keep your head up as you carry out the move gently and smoothly. It is best for you and for the person you are caring for if you can manage to stay relaxed.

Figure 1 Placing your feet for a stable base

The simple motto of the organisation BackCare is 'Think BACK before you ACT'. In the Appendix to this book is an extract from BackCare's *Safer Handling of People in the Community*.

Practical equipment

If you have difficulty in managing certain tasks, there may be gadgets or equipment that can help you. For example: there are special taps for people who have difficulty using ordinary ones; amplifiers for telephones

35

or televisions, for people with hearing difficulties; magnifiers for partially sighted people; aids to help people pull themselves out of bed, or to put on stockings. There are many more aids, including wheelchairs, sticks, commodes, special non-slip trays and bath seats. There is a huge range of gadgets and equipment designed to make everyday life easier for disabled people and their carers. Here we look at:

■ where you can get support aids and equipment;
■ where you can view them or try them out;
■ help with paying for them.

Case study

John said:

'They gave us an Oxford hoist and a sling in the beginning to help move my dad when he had a stroke and first came out of hospital. But you don't really know what you are going to need for about a month until you try it out.

'The hoist was one you are supposed to be able to move about from room to room but it was very heavy, especially on carpets, and my mum couldn't manage it. So we bought an overhead electric hoist to put over the bed and another in the sitting room. We couldn't get it on the NHS but it made life a lot easier. We also had to have a level-access shower put in and we paid for that because they said there was a three-year waiting list. The shower chair by itself was £600 but that was very useful as we could put it over the toilet as well ... it's like a wheelchair but it has a hole in the seat. The only problem with the one we bought was that it was difficult to turn, as only the front wheels turned. Then we got a really good occupational therapist (OT) – one who was really helpful – and she got us a different shower chair which had all four wheels that turned and it was much easier to use. Finding someone like her was a real godsend but we had to wait ages for an assessment. The sad thing was that Dad had an assessment by the hospital OT but when they passed us over to social services they wouldn't accept the hospital OT's decision and put us on the waiting list for another assessment.

'With the sling ... it was hurting my dad when we used it as it pulled on his arms. We found a firm that came out and measured him and looked at the problem and made a sling with two extra strings that made it much more comfortable for him to use.

'Then there was the catheter. It was a real problem because it kept getting blocked. So in the end I rang up the company that made them and asked them for advice. They told me that the one we'd been given wasn't meant for long-term use – it was just a cheap disposable one, costing £3 or so – that was meant to be used for less than a week. So we got the more expensive kind, which cost about £10 a time but lasted longer ... and it was much less of a problem, though there was always the risk of infection. Later I found out there is a different system for men that is not invasive at all – it fits over, instead. That's more expensive still, of course, but much better for him. So cost was obviously a factor in determining which equipment we were given.

'I believe that we might get Direct Payments for equipment in the future but it hasn't happened here yet. Then I would be able to choose the right equipment.'

Local authorities now *must* offer Direct Payments. You can get help and advice from CarersLine (contact details on page 262) or from your local:

- disability organisations
- carers' projects
- social services department (social work department in Scotland; Health and Social Services Trust in Northern Ireland).

For medical support aids and equipment, your GP is the first point of contact and a key person in referring you to other professionals. You can also contact the social services office for your area by finding it in the telephone book under the name of your local authority. Services vary widely from place to place; some will be free but for others there may be a small charge. The Table on pages 38 and 39 gives you an idea of what help may be available from statutory and voluntary agencies and whom to contact.

Sources of practical help and equipment

Help	Source
Home nursing equipment, continence advice and supplies, bed accessories	Community nurse or continence adviser (ask GP for a referral)
Stoma products	GP or primary care team
Equipment to manage diabetes	GP or primary care team
Wound and support dressings	GP or primary care team
Respiratory equipment	GP or primary care team
Laundry	Private companies (look in *Yellow Pages*)
Mobility and exercise advice	District nurse, physiotherapist, occupational therapist (ask GP for a referral)
Small equipment and advice to help with everyday living (eg washing, cooking, using the toilet); raised or special bed	Occupational therapist (ask GP or social services for a referral)
Handrails, ramps, hoists and other small adaptations to the home	Occupational therapist (ask GP or social services for a referral)
Mobility aids (eg wheelchair, walking stick, walking frame, footwear appliances)	Physiotherapist, chiropodist, podiatrist, or occupational therapist (ask GP, hospital consultant or social services)
Short-term hire of equipment	Age Concern day centres, other voluntary organisations (eg British Red Cross, WRVS)
Larger adaptations to your home, such as wider doorways, changes to the bathroom, installing a lift, bath and bed hoists	Occupational therapist (ask GP or social services), local housing department or voluntary organisation (eg Foundations or Care and Repair), private companies

(Continued)

Local transport assistance	Voluntary organisations or private taxi companies
Adapted car, scooter or wheelchair	Motability (Department for Work and Pensions)
Disabled person's parking badge	Local authority
Emergency response alarm system	Local authority or voluntary organisation (eg Age Concern or the Disabled Living Foundation)
Equipment for people who have a hearing problem	Hospital consultant, phone company, voluntary organisations (eg RNID), social services
Equipment for people who have a sight problem	Hospital consultant, voluntary organisations (eg RNIB), social services
Educational equipment	Education authority or board
Employment equipment (eg special computers, talking calculators, loud-speaker telephone accessories)	Department for Work and Pensions – employment service

Note Contact details of the organisations listed can be found in the 'Useful addresses' section.

> ### Case study
>
> **Nancy** said:
>
> 'Mobility is absolutely vital. We've got one of those badges for parking the car but my husband can't go by himself as I'm the driver. I also have to watch out for the different rules in each of the towns we go to. In one place we go you can park anywhere, even on double yellow lines for as long as you like. In another town, although you can park only in the marked bays, there are lots of them and you can stay as long as you like. But here you can park only in the marked bays for a maximum of three hours and there aren't many marked bays. So I have to watch out as it's easy to forget.'

There are a number of companies that sell support aids and equipment. Many have a mail order service for people who are unable to visit their showrooms. Before you buy, it is a good idea to get unbiased advice from the appropriate therapist.

Coping with difficult conditions

There are some circumstances in which the caring role can become more complex. When you are dealing with someone who has a condition that is difficult to manage, you may need extra help. The conditions that we consider here are: forgetfulness, wandering, aggression and incontinence. Many of these behaviours are associated with dementia but may also occur with other conditions.

The diseases that cause dementia are more common in older people but dementia is not a normal part of ageing. The term 'dementia' describes a group of symptoms that result from destruction of the brain cells. For more detailed information, contact Alzheimer's Society (details on page 229).

Although dementia is a physical illness, most of the symptoms and problems caused by it require psychiatric expertise and care. Dementia gradually affects the ability of people to:

- remember things for more than a few seconds;
- make sense of the world around them;
- cope with the daily tasks of living;
- express their feelings;
- take the initiative or make plans;
- think clearly and solve problems;
- cope with an over-stimulating environment;
- behave in the normal ways they have learned during their lives.

No two people are alike and different people may develop different symptoms, depending on their personality and the nature of the illness. Common symptoms include:

- Memory loss – an early sign indistinguishable from forgetfulness brought on through stress or depression. This can result in getting lost because the person forgets the way back home. It can show itself in repetition of conversations or actions.
- Changes in personality – mild-mannered people may become abusive or aggressive. Some people lose their social inhibitions, take up swearing and behave in ways that they would formerly have regarded as outrageous. Others become more sweet natured and passive.
- Difficulty in communicating – names of objects and people cannot be recalled. The person may have difficulty in making themselves understood or in understanding what is said (eg instructions or explanations). This can be misinterpreted as unco-operative behaviour.
- Loss of practical skills – simple tasks such as unbuttoning a shirt can become impossible. Daily activities such as feeding, dressing and washing can become more difficult as the illness progresses.

Most forms of dementia are irreversible and, eventually, fatal. Physical treatment is limited and the length of time the person lives with the condition depends a lot on their general health and the age at which they develop the disease. However, much can be done to help manage the illness, so it is essential to get advice from the GP. It is also possible now to control the early stages of Alzheimer's, so prompt diagnosis is important … while understanding that occasional lapses of memory do not indicate early dementia.

Caring for someone with dementia can be very stressful but you may become accustomed to the demands of a person who cannot hold an ordinary conversation and sometimes forgets who you are. But the later stages of dementia present new problems. Changes in personality and behaviour can create new stresses that develop gradually over a period of time and, as carer, you become more and more tired and less able to cope. Pat has dementia and presented Peter with all the difficult conditions listed above.

Case study

Peter said:

'I was in the Navy so I'm used to routine and that's how I coped with looking after Pat. I always got up at the same time, rallied her and got her ready for the day. We had breakfast and then, because of the medication she was on, she would go back to sleep in the big armchair. After a while, if I needed something at the corner shop, I had the confidence to leave her for a few moments while she was asleep … she couldn't fall out. Then I would make lunch … she would eat anything by then, which was a help to me. Before she was ill she was a very faddy eater but all that went, along with everything else. Her behaviour changed a lot in that respect.

'Constipation was a bit of a problem if I wasn't careful to make sure she ate the right things to help that. I think the routine helped me deal with the continence problems. She always went at the same time every day if we stuck to our routine. The continence nurse came to visit us and gave me some advice. She was good and we got our supply of free pads every two months … two pads each day plus a big one for night time.

'I took up the carpets when the incontinence started as it was just easier to wash the tiles and keep the place smelling good. Then I found I had to put a lock on the kitchen door; otherwise, she would go in and turn the gas on and break stuff if I took my eye off her for a moment. I was afraid she would blow us all up or cut herself on the broken glass while I was in the shower. You pretty soon learn that you've got to put everything dangerous out of harm's way. The outside doors were the same … after she went off down the road a couple of times and neighbours had to bring her back, I decided we had to lock ourselves in to be on the safe side.

'Once Pat couldn't get about much, she spent most of the day in the big armchair. It was comfortable for her to sit in and she couldn't fall out … and I could wheel it about. To make that easier, I decided to take up the carpets and put down tiles throughout. I'm a carpenter so I can do lots of things myself. I took the doors off their hinges so I could get from one room to another easier … and I put up some partitions to make like a bed-sitting room for Pat. We spent most of the day in there when we weren't out. There was her chair and her bed and the television and a couple of radiators to make sure she was warm enough. I had to heat that room even if we didn't heat the rest so much. We've got a big ground floor flat … it's rented but the landlord was fine about me making alterations. He's always been very supportive.

'Every day after lunch we would get dressed up and I'd take her out in the wheel-chair. That was one of the big things that I think was different for her, not being in a care home. I made sure she got fresh air and a change of scene every day and I got the exercise I needed, too. Sometimes people are reluctant to go out if they are stigmatised in some way. It's like they are ashamed and don't want people to see them but I wouldn't be doing with any of that. I think if these are the cards you are dealt with then you just have to get on with it. I took her everywhere. I took her to Carers meetings too … she was looked after while we had our meeting. There are lots of volunteers at the Centre … most of them ex-carers so they know what to do. Not feeling isolated is vital, so the meetings are very important. When I took her to the hospital for appointments and it looked like there was going to be a wait I would explain to the others: 'My wife's got Alzheimer's. It's going to be difficult for her to wait. Do you mind if we go in next?' So we jumped the queue and they never minded. It's no good just sitting there if you can do something about it, is there?

'I used to dress her in jogging tops and sports socks and sweat shirts because they're easy to get on and off and easy to wash if they get wet. Sometimes you have to change them several times a day so you need something practical and warm. When she didn't know who I was I had to find ways of getting her clothes off and on without frightening her … because I was a stranger to her, she thought she was being attacked. But I found that if I put my arms round her and gave her a cuddle I could slip her clothes off without her minding too much. Otherwise, she would resist … so I got to learn her body language, too. I had to know how to approach her to get her to co-operate.

'At the end of the day we spent time sitting together watching whatever was on the television; she was back in bed by 8 but I sat with her till I went to bed myself. Respite was vital … it recharges your batteries. You can carry on longer if you can get a break. I found it distressing to leave her at the respite centre at first but when I saw that she seemed happy I relaxed about it. I gained the confidence to leave her there. I sometimes thought she recognised the Unit manager there more than me … perhaps she thought he was her husband. She followed him around when she could still walk and didn't like the other patients talking to him … but you have to learn to get used to that.'

As Peter explained, he had to find ways to manage incontinence, Pat's changed personality, her personal safety and so on long after she had ceased to know that he was her husband. The ways he managed the daily business of caring included:

- appropriate clothes;
- routine to manage continence;
- outings to get fresh air and exercise;
- maintaining social contacts;
- respite care;
- adjusting their environment to take safety into account;
- learning to recognise and respond to Pat's body language and behaviour;
- accepting things he couldn't change.

It is important to distinguish between caring about and caring for. Caring *about* someone means wanting to give them what we all want:

as much freedom and independence as possible for as long as possible. Caring *for* someone is more complicated and most people, while they enjoy being cared for from time to time, would not want to be cared for all the time. Most of us prefer to be in control of our own lives. Being a carer can be very hard work but being cared for also has its frustrations and problems.

Case study

Margaret found that her own heart condition made it much harder to keep up with her husband's wanderings.

'He would go rushing off, and I would hurry after him as best I could. But I just couldn't keep up. Once, I collapsed on my neighbours' doorstep. I was so breathless I could hardly get my words out. When they realised what had happened, they went after him in the car and brought him back. Another time he went out wearing his carpet slippers in the pouring rain and he fell down near the church. I managed to get him back and into dry clothes. But I couldn't cope so I started locking the doors to stop him rushing off. After that, we lived behind locked doors, which was heartbreaking.'

It is very difficult to get the right balance between maintaining safety and giving someone you care about their freedom and their right to take risks.

Making a home a safer environment

If you were employed as a carer, your employer would be responsible for ensuring that your workplace was safe. When you take on the role of carer either in your home or in the home of the person you care for, you have to take responsibility for your own safety. You will also want to make the environment as safe as possible for the person you are looking after. If you or the person you care for pay carers who come into your house, you have responsibilities for their health and safety, as other employers do, under the Health and Safety at Work Act and other similar legislation.

Risk assessment is the formal way in which employers manage health and safety.

- A **hazard** is something that has the potential to cause harm.
- When you assess the **risk** associated with that hazard, you examine the likelihood that someone will be harmed by that hazard and how severe the outcome is likely to be.

In assessing whether there are any hazards in your home, you have to take into account the particular characteristics of the people who live there; for example, a gas cooker can be a hazard if the person using it is likely to turn on the gas and forget to light it. But it does not represent a particular hazard worth worrying about when used by the average person. So, taking this example further, in deciding whether you need to take any action about the gas cooker you have to consider how likely it is that it will be misused in some way that could result in an explosion. You could decide to change to electricity for cooking or arrange for meals to be delivered instead of having to be cooked. If there is always a carer in the house, you might decide that it is not a hazard that you need to take any action on.

Below is a checklist you could take round the house with you to help identify hazards. As well as looking in each room, check other parts of the home, including stairs, and outbuildings (eg sheds).

Home safety checklist

Potential hazard	Is any action necessary and if so what?
Gas appliances	Have them checked regularly; some devices will turn themselves off if left unlit; there are also gas detectors
Loose mats and rugs	Remove or fix in place securely
Staircase	Make sure carpet is properly fitted and that there are rails both sides if needed
	(Continued)

Medicines and poisons (eg cleaning materials and bleach)	Must be clearly labelled and out of harm's way
Level of lighting	May need higher power light bulbs in corridors and staircases; extra lamps can be used to light dark corners
Height of cupboards or shelves	Minimise necessity to reach, bend or lift awkwardly by moving the cupboards or leaving them empty
Food	Discard waste food safely; keep surfaces hygienic; check temperature of refrigerator and re-heated food; do not re-freeze thawed food
Bathroom	Use non slip mats; replace bath with shower
Hot water	Use the thermostat to make sure no one can be scalded by water from the tap; use a safe design of kettle in a safe place
Fire	Smoke alarms need regular maintenance, as do fire extinguishers. A fire blanket may be useful in the kitchen. Open fires or heaters may need a guard. Smokers can pose a real fire risk
Unwelcome visitors to the house/intruders	Use a chain on the front door; carry a personal alarm; fit stout locks and a burglar alarm system
Glass doors	Should be safety glass or covered with shatter-proof film
Electric wiring	Have wiring checked by an electrician; make sure sockets and fuses are not overloaded; get rid of trailing flexes

The house needs to be the right temperature, and good insulation will help you achieve this along with efficient heating systems. Energywatch (see your phone book) can help you find the company in your area that provides gas and electricity at the most economical cost.

Case study

Annie said:

'I think my role is about:

- providing support;
- providing stability;
- providing reassurance;
- providing stimulation;
- ensuring a safe, secure environment: we looked at our home from the point of view of is there anything he could trip over or bang into; can he reach everything he needs when I'm not here. He walks with a stick so he can do some things for himself;
- promoting and encouraging independence – it is important to let him do as much as possible for himself without putting himself at risk;
- promoting communication: communication is vital – it is so easy to take over. I make sure the health and social care professionals talk to both of us although I usually make the first move. When we are going to meet someone, we discuss before we go what we need to find out and how we are going to handle things.

'Being a carer is very demanding and stressful, so you have to develop coping strategies in the home and outside it.

'When I'm here, my keys are always in the door and the doors are not locked but Malcolm has his own set, too. One of the most important things we did was get a telephone for every room so that if I'm not here Malcolm can reach one whichever room he's in. I carry a mobile, too, and I phone from time to time to make sure he's okay. There are emergency numbers written up, too, so he can see them easily.

'On a day-to-day basis it is important not to feel you have to do everything your-self. Independence is so important.

'With medication we have a daily dosage system that comes in a tray so you can see if you've taken all the pills for that day. Malcolm is able to manage his own medication but I do just check that he's taken them all because it is so easy to forget. Then we keep the medicines locked up in a safe place so the grand-children can't get at them and also because someone who is very ill can get depressed and you don't want to leave temptation in their way. I make sure we get repeat prescriptions a week ahead so we never run out. Our GP is very help-ful and will always come if we need him.

'We plan our menus a week at a time and we each have a copy so Malcolm always knows what we're eating that day. He can take food out of the fridge if I put it on the top shelf, so I encourage him to do some food preparation under supervision. He can take a meal out of the fridge and put it in the oven for me if I'm working late. He had great difficulty holding utensils and things at first so we got some special gadgets – plate rings and grip handles – which helped a lot. Our local chemist shop has quite a good list of gadgets and supplies for caring for someone at home.

'Malcolm set up his own rehabilitation when he came home – he walks up and down while he's here and picks things up and squeezes them – and worked out his own pattern of exercise. He's done really well. He lives for his newspaper – reads it from cover to cover and does the crossword. Then he watches TV. He also does his bit for the community by sitting on a stool at the window to do his shift for Neighbourhood Watch.

'I think it's important to see the outside world as well. We have a day out every two weeks – out for lunch or even just sit in the park. We go on the bus – we've got those low level ones here but I have to help him on. The drivers have been really good because he could fall over if they start suddenly before he's sitting down.

'I need time for myself too, and Malcolm understands that. You have to take care of yourself; otherwise, you can't care for someone else. It's really important to feel appreciated too, not taken for granted – I say to him 'I need to know that you appreciate what I'm doing.' … and he does. He's good like that … thanks me and makes me feel better. I get a lot of good words from the grandchildren too – they understand what I'm doing and they're pleased that I'm looking after their granddad.

'Sometimes I just need to relax or go shopping or socialise. Malcolm has a copy of my working hours for the week, so he knows where I am and we discuss each week and plan ahead. I go out with the grandchildren sometimes and our daughter or daughter-in-law, or sometimes I go to a concert with my friend. One of the family will always come and sit with him if I've arranged to go out and he's not well or something.

'The family visit us sometimes and we go on holiday. We're going to Scotland soon on the train to stay with friends. I phone the disability line before we travel by train and they make sure they have someone at the station to help. If we go on a coach trip I do the same – phone up and arrange for him to have a seat in a convenient place. They are always very good like that. We've got a short break away with friends and then we're going away on our own for a few days in September. We always stay in the same cottage, so we know the house and the area, and we'll do a bit of walking.'

Key points

- Carers find a variety of ways of dealing with the everyday business of living and caring.

- It is important for the person you care for to take as much responsibility as possible for their own medication.

- Food has a special place in our lives, which goes far beyond its nutritional function.

- Regular simple exercise in the context of healthy eating and living can help to maintain our ability to function.

- Looking after your back is vital.

- If you provide personal help with toileting and bathing, including physically demanding tasks, you need professional advice about moving someone from one place to another without damaging yourself.

- If you have difficulty in managing certain tasks, there may be gadgets, aids or equipment that can help you.

- Some equipment can be borrowed free. If you buy equipment, it is a good idea to get unbiased advice from the appropriate therapist.

- When you are dealing with someone who has a condition that is difficult to manage, the caring role can become more complex and you may need extra help.

- When you take on the role of carer either in your home or in the home of the person you care for, you have to take responsibility for your own safety and think about the safety of the person you care for.

- Caring about someone means wanting to give them what we all want: as much freedom and independence as possible for as long as possible. Most of us prefer to be in control of our own lives.

- Being a carer can be very hard work but being cared for also has its frustrations and problems.

3 Coping with a crisis

In the past it was usually a telegram that brought bad news. Nowadays it is more likely to be a telephone call that alerts you to a crisis. It might be a call from a relative or neighbour, or from the hospital where your relative or friend has been admitted. It could be a sudden illness or an accident. Perhaps a long-standing condition such as cancer or Alzheimer's disease has become worse. Or the person who usually carries out the caring role has fallen ill or had an accident.

In this chapter we look at how to deal with common health crises and difficult situations such as:

- mental health crisis
- heart attack
- stroke
- dementia
- cancer
- fractures
- falls
- living with pain
- hypoglycaemia/hyperglycaemia.

Your first reaction to a crisis or difficult situation may well be one of panic, especially if the call is unexpected or comes late at night.

However upset you feel, try to remain calm. It will help you to think more clearly. (Try some of the techniques outlined in Chapter 7 to help you calm down.)

Case study

Julie's story:

'It was six o'clock one evening when I heard about my mother's accident. I was just getting the tea on the table. Peter had got back late and tired from work. The twins were demanding attention. It was one of those days. Then there was a phone call from the hospital in Cleveland, saying my mother had had a bad fall and broken her leg.

'I just panicked. "Right," I said, "I'm off! I've got to get up there. I'm bringing her back with me. She can't go on living alone."

'Peter calmed me down. "Sit down," he said, "and finish your tea. Let's talk this through. I've got nothing against your mother living with us, if it's the best thing for everybody. But we can't just rush into a big decision like this."

'Over tea we talked over the possibilities. Peter said, "Why don't you phone your brother in Newcastle. It's much nearer for him. He could go up tonight and you can go up tomorrow."

'I phoned my brother. He'd also heard from the hospital and was just about to set off. "I'll be there in half an hour," he said, "but I can't stay next day because of work." I said I would go up the next day and we agreed to get together later on and have a talk. I arranged for a neighbour to pick up the twins from school next day and I went up on the train.

'I was glad I phoned my brother. I'd never been very close to him, and somehow I didn't think he'd be much help. In fact, looking after Mother has brought us closer together, and now we share caring for her.'

Julie found that in this kind of crisis it was sensible to take a while to think through the options before making any decisions.

Deciding what to do now and what can wait

There is no need to make big decisions on the spur of the moment. For one thing, in the event of sudden illness or accident, the patient's condition will keep changing from day to day. Julie was glad she phoned her brother because it helped her to take a more measured approach to the problem. It is much better to wait until the condition has stabilised so that you have a clearer idea of future care needs and ability to live independently. Waiting a bit also gives you time to adjust to the situation. You might feel shocked and upset to begin with but after a day or two in hospital things may look much better. Take your time and talk to everyone involved so that you can make a measured judgement.

Assessing the immediate situation

There will probably be certain decisions you need to make immediately, depending on the circumstances. If the crisis is happening some way away from you, do you need to call an ambulance or get someone else to sit with the patient until you arrive? Start by collecting as much information as you can, by ringing back if necessary when you have had time to think. The sorts of questions you might want to ask include:

- Is medical help required and if so what level – eg GP or ambulance?
- Can your relative or friend phone for medical help or will someone else need to do it?
- Can your relative or friend get up from a chair or the bed (or the floor) to make a drink, answer the door or go to the toilet?
- Is there a neighbour who could be asked to come round? If so, does the neighbour already have a key to get in?
- Are there worrying symptoms, such as pain, dizziness, breathlessness, drowsiness, bleeding or possible broken bones?
- Is your relative or friend worried about being alone until help arrives?

If someone else is already there, that will make the situation less alarming for you. In an emergency, the police have the authority to break into a house where someone is in difficulties and cannot answer the door.

The crisis flowchart shown in Figure 2 should help to guide you through the things you need to do immediately.

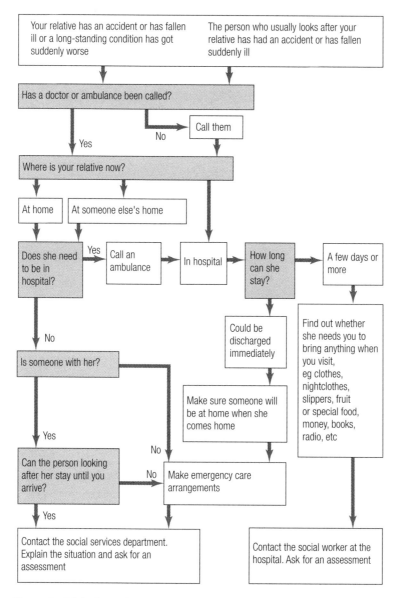

Figure 2 Crisis flow-chart

Case study

Penny told us about how she and her husband cope with the crises in their daughter's mental health.

'If someone has an enduring mental health problem such as schizophrenia, when they are well they are usually happy to accept help from people but when they start to become ill, one of the signs is refusing help, turning against their carers and professionals. That makes a crisis very difficult to manage.

'What happened a few weeks ago was that Paula's CPN (community psychiatric nurse; now often called "community mental health nurse") was off sick; there was no one to cover her work so no one was checking that Paula was taking her medication. We realised something was wrong when she wouldn't let us or anybody else in. In the end we had to get the police so they could get into the house … and she could be "sectioned" (compulsorily admitted to hospital, under section 2 of the Mental Health Act) … and forced to take her medication. It has happened before, of course, so we are familiar now with how it works … but it is horrible; even though it is for her own good, it makes us feel awful … I dread it happening and I often get a reaction afterwards – become physically ill myself.

'One of the good things that's happened lately, though, is a new system called an Advance Directive. It is an agreement that Paula wrote and signed when she was well which we, as her carers, and all the professionals can use when there is a crisis. The Advance Directive provides information about Paula's views on her mental health care and the treatment she would prefer to have in the event that she becomes unwell … because then of course she can't make informed choices. It also has information about other things such as pets … and other things that are important in someone's personal and home life. It doesn't have full legal status but it is very helpful for all of us.'

The Advance Directive is mentioned in the National Service Framework for mental health and in the National Institute for Clinical Excellence (NICE) guidelines on schizophrenia but each area can design their own version (see Chapter 4 for more details).

Arranging care in a crisis

In an emergency, it is possible that you could drop everything and just go. But for most people this is not feasible, whether in the short term or the long term, because of other commitments. This may mean you have to arrange short-term emergency care with a view to making longer term arrangements in due course if that becomes necessary. It is important to plan ahead so that you know whom you can call on to help in a crisis. Possibilities include:

■ Other members of the family who live nearby or might be able to provide care in the short term.

■ A friend or neighbour of your relative.

■ The GP.

■ The local social services department – there should be a 24-hour emergency number and a duty officer who will take the details and arrange for an assessment, or, failing that, should be able to put you in touch with other emergency care arrangements.

■ For someone who is in hospital, talk to the hospital discharge team; they may include health care staff and social services care managers, depending on where your relative lives.

■ Carers UK helpline for information about caring services.

■ There may be a voluntary organisation in your area providing care in people's own homes (eg Crossroads). Check whether there is a charge – it might be free. They should be registered with the Commission for Social Care Inspection (CSCI).

■ There will probably be private agencies in your area providing care for people in their own homes. There will be a charge but if social services carry out an assessment and agree that the service is necessary, there might be financial assistance, depending on your relative's financial circumstances. The UK Home Care Association (contact details on page 256) should have a list of agencies. They should also be registered with the CSCI.

- Local Age Concerns and other voluntary organisations that support carers will know about services available in your area and may have a network of volunteer visitors who could help.
- Nursing agencies provide trained nurses who can go into people's own homes. Fees vary from area to area. They should also be registered with the CSCI.

First aid

First aid is the initial treatment given after an accident or when someone has been taken ill unexpectedly. It can improve someone's chances of recovery and sometimes saves lives. Anyone can go on a first aid training course and many of the carers who helped us in the preparation of this book said how helpful they had found such a course. As well as showing you what to do in an emergency, the trainer also advises on the sorts of things you should keep in the medicine cupboard and consider taking with you when you go on an outing in the car (eg bandages and sterile dressings). One of the important things they will show you is how to put someone into a safe position – called the recovery position (Figure 3) – if they are lying on the floor, so that they won't choke. Mouth-to-mouth resuscitation is another life-saving skill that you can learn.

Figure 3 The recovery position

Common health crises in older people

In this section we look at some of the health problems that are most common in older people and which may require emergency treatment, creating a crisis situation for family or friends. We look at dementia, heart attack, stroke, cancer, falls and the hypoglycaemia/hypergly-caemia (low/high blood sugar) associated with diabetes.

Although dementia develops gradually over a number of years, it is included here because it is often a crisis – an accident at home, sudden illness, or the person wandering away and getting lost – that alerts the family to the need to take action. Cancer, too, often develops gradually, particularly in older people. But there may be points in the course of the disease when a crisis occurs, for example when it is first diagnosed and immediate treatment is necessary, or in the final stages.

Case study

Roy realised his father was getting a bit absent-minded and strange in his ways, but he didn't think anything of it until one night he was woken up by a knock at the door. It was the police. They had Roy's father in the back of the car. He was in his pyjamas and dressing gown.

'They'd picked Dad up wandering along the edge of the motorway. He said he'd lost his way. We were horrified to realise the danger he'd been in.

'We'd always thought he was quite happy living on his own. My wife or I would drop by every day. And he had good neighbours who kept an eye on him after Mum died. They did tell us he would occasionally knock on their door late at night, but they always made him a cup of tea and sent him home. This time they were away and we think he must have set out to try to find us. Thank goodness the police picked him up before anything happened.

'We realised he wouldn't be able to live on his own any longer, but we really had no idea what to do. We put him to bed in our room and my wife and I bedded down on the sofa downstairs. We didn't get much sleep. We spent the whole night talking about what to do.

'The police told us to contact social services and they sent someone round next day. They said it would be best if he went into a care home. Dad was very upset at that idea. He said we were locking him away. But after he'd been to see the home he perked up a bit. He likes company and there were plenty of people to talk to. There's even someone on duty at night if he feels like taking a midnight wander.'

Some people with dementia manage to live in their own homes for quite a long time, with support from their family, social services and primary care team. After a while, however, it can become too risky for them to live on their own. It often happens that a sudden crisis, such as an accident or illness, makes us aware that they can no longer cope alone.

Staying independent

If your relative wishes to continue living in their own home alone, it is important to minimise the risks of doing so. But it is impossible to take away all risks without forfeiting the person's own dignity and independence. The level of acceptable risk can become an issue that family members disagree about. There may be misunderstandings, unrealistic assumptions or unnecessary fears. There are a number of measures you can take to minimise risk:

- Medicines and poisons – lock away cleaning fluids or other household poisons and make sure medication is supervised in some way.
- Fire – smokers pose a real fire risk. Make sure that smoke detectors are fitted and that fires or heaters have guards.
- Gas – sometimes gas can be turned on and left unlit, which is very dangerous. If this happens, some alternative may have to be arranged; for example, change the fuel used for cooking and/or heating, arrange for meals to be delivered instead of having to be cooked. But removing the need to cook meals may in itself be disorientating

and leave an important gap in the daily routine. There are also gas detectors that could be useful if someone visits the house regularly.

■ Falls – check the house for dangerous surfaces – slippery floors, loose carpets etc. Get advice about aids and adaptations, such as bath mat, bath seat and handrails. Make sure the light levels are right.

■ Locks – perhaps locks on internal doors should be removed so that the person cannot get locked in the bathroom accidentally and can be rescued easily in the event of an accident. Keep a set of duplicate keys so that you can enter in an emergency.

■ Warmth – ensure the house is well insulated (this may be grant aided) and heating is adequate.

■ Talk to neighbours and friends – ask them to keep an eye open, and leave your phone number with them so they can contact you.

For more information see *Caring for someone with dementia* by Jane Brotchie, published by Age Concern.

Heart attack

A sudden heart attack happens when the blood supply to part of the heart is suddenly blocked by a blood clot, or thrombus.

Case study

Mina said:

'It came as a shock when my husband, Jay, had a heart attack. He was only 62 and had always seemed so fit and well, even if he did smoke a bit more than he should. He'd been complaining about pains in his chest a few days before but I didn't think anything of it. I thought it was just indigestion. Then suddenly he crumpled up with this terrible pain in his chest.

'I phoned the ambulance and fortunately they were pretty quick. They got him into hospital and wired him up to all sorts of hi-tech machines. He looked so pitiful lying there with wires stuck all over him. What amazed me was the way they had him out of bed and walking about again so quickly. I thought it was a bit cruel but apparently that's what they do nowadays because it's better to get people up and moving about.

'At first I was just relieved he was still alive. And with all the fuss and attention he was getting we didn't really think about the future. Then they moved him off the special cardiac ward on to the general ward. He was with a lot of old men – at least they seemed old – and he started to get depressed and anxious. "I don't look as old as them, do I, Mina?" he'd say. Of course I reassured him, but the truth was that my view of him had changed. I'd always thought of him as the strong one in our relationship. Now I was seeing the vulnerable side of him.

'When he came home, it was even harder. He would swing from being optimistic and full of plans to being down in the dumps. The doctor told me I should encourage him to do things for himself, not wait on him hand and foot. He said it was important to build up Jay's independence. But I felt so mean.

'The best thing was the doctor telling him he had to stop smoking and start regular exercise. He recommended walking. We started going out into the countryside during the week, when there was no one else around. Sometimes we would set out early and stop for a pub lunch. We discovered lovely places we'd never known about. And it brought us closer together again. We were like a young couple walking through the fields holding hands.

'Yes, the heart attack has changed our lives, but it's had some good effects. Jay is not as caught up in his work as he used to be … he realises there are other things in life.'

Recognising a heart attack

The arteries that supply the heart are called the coronary arteries. A clot in one of these arteries is called a coronary thrombosis, which (like 'myocardial infarction') is another name for a heart attack. A heart attack is more likely to happen if the arteries are clogged with a fatty substance called atheroma. This restricts the free circulation of the blood and makes clotting more likely. If the coronary arteries are severely clogged, people sometimes get a chest pain called angina. This is a warning sign that a heart attack could happen. But often a heart attack happens without any warning at all. Smoking, high blood pressure, diabetes or unusually high cholesterol levels are all factors that contribute to the build-up of atheroma and make a heart attack more likely.

What to do if someone has a heart attack

A heart attack is a serious medical emergency, so never delay in calling an ambulance. A single tablet of aspirin is a useful immediate treatment that can be given at home, provided the person is conscious, is not sensitive to aspirin and can swallow without difficulty. If the following symptoms are present, dial 999:

■ Pain – crushing, squeezing, pressing – starting in the central chest and radiating outward into the neck, shoulders and arms.
■ Paleness with cold sweats.
■ Breathlessness.
■ Palpitations (usually rapid and strong heart beat).
■ Nausea and vomiting.
■ Faintness or partial loss of consciousness.

Paramedic teams are trained to give excellent care for a suspected heart attack and will start emergency treatment before the person reaches hospital. Make your relative lie down if they are not already doing so. Stay with them for reassurance and to check any changes in their condition. If they stop breathing, give mouth-to-mouth resuscitation. Cardiac massage should be given only by someone trained in the technique.

Case study

Fiona, a doctor, says:

'The sooner the diagnosis of the heart attack is made, the better – the sooner treatment is started, the more likely it is to be effective.'

Someone with a suspected heart attack will be taken either direct to a coronary care unit (CCU) or to an accident and emergency (A&E) centre, depending on the bed space and hospital facilities in your area. Initially a diagnosis is made from a description of the pain. Tests are done at a later stage to confirm the preliminary diagnosis and to determine the extent of damage to the heart muscle.

The care of people who have had a heart attack differs according to their individual needs and the practice favoured by different consultants. But all treatments work towards early mobility and discharge from hospital. For more information on after care see *Caring for someone with a heart problem* by Toni Battison, published by Age Concern, and all the leaflets published by the British Heart Foundation (contact details on page 232).

Stroke

A stroke happens when arteries supplying blood to the brain either get blocked (thrombosis) or burst causing bleeding (haemorrhage). This cuts off the blood supply to part of the brain and, without oxygen and nutrients, brain cells stop working and then die. Each group of cells has a specialised function. This means that after a stroke the person can no longer perform the functions that those brain cells used to control. Every stroke has different effects, depending on which part of the brain is damaged and how severely. The most common effect is partial paralysis and loss of feeling on one side of the body – the opposite side to the part of the brain that is damaged. Memory, reading and writing, understanding, emotions, balance, walking, speech, vision, continence and other bodily functions can be affected, though usually not all together.

Recognising a stroke

The symptoms of stroke vary enormously but often involve weakness or paralysis of the face, arm or leg and some loss of speech. About one-third of people remain fully conscious throughout, another third become confused and the final third become unconscious. Other common effects are difficulty in swallowing and changes in the sense of touch or feeling. A stroke can happen anywhere and at any time but most occur at home. About one person in five has a stroke while they are sleeping. Most people can tell you what is happening to them but about a third lose the ability to speak. About one person in twenty has a fit (convulsion).

Sometimes the signs of a stroke appear and then rapidly get better within a few hours. This happens when the blood supply to the brain is briefly cut off but then restored. This is called a transient ischaemic attack, or TIA, and is a warning sign.

How to recognise a TIA

The following symptoms may occur separately or in combination:

- blindness or blind spots in one eye or both;
- difficulty in talking;
- double vision and other distortions of sight;
- left-sided blindness or right-sided blindness in both eyes;
- numbness, weakness or tingling of an arm, leg, hand or foot or one side of the face or body;
- dizziness (vertigo).

If your relative has a TIA, it is important to see a doctor because prompt treatment can prevent a later complete stroke, with irreversible brain damage. Strokes are common in people who have high blood pressure, heart disease or diabetes or are over 75. Smoking, being overweight, taking little exercise and drinking too much alcohol all add to the risk.

What to do when someone has a stroke

Always give first aid first; then get medical help.

- If the person is unconscious, put them into the 'recovery position': on one side with the head tilted backwards. This ensures that the person will not choke if they are sick. Get help from someone else to do this if you need to – don't leave the person on their back.

- Be careful not to pull on a paralysed limb; this can damage muscle, bones or joints. Hold or move the person using the trunk.
- If the person has a fit, just make sure there is a clear space around with no furniture or sharp objects to cause injury.
- If the person is conscious, just provide reassurance and comfort.
- Phone an ambulance or the person's GP.

Although doctors can do little in the first stages to limit the extent of a stroke or to speed recovery, they can help prevent further complications. The decision whether to call an ambulance or the GP depends on:

- the seriousness of the stroke;
- your ability to provide care at home;
- your confidence in the GP.

Hospital may be the best option if:

- the person is unconscious;
- there is a fit lasting more than two minutes;
- the doctor is not sure of the diagnosis and wants further tests to be carried out;
- there is no one to provide care at home.

Case study

Emily's mother was fit and active until she had a stroke, which left her paralysed down one side and unable to use her right arm. She then came to live with Emily and her family and stayed for the next 20 years.

'She had always been a very active woman and I knew I had to keep her busy and cheerful. She would still knit and iron with one hand. If I was cooking something I would pass her the spoon and say "Stir this for me, Mum".

'I think the grandchildren kept her going. They behaved as though there was nothing different about her. We all tried to keep her cheerful and optimistic – I think that's very important. I was lucky to have a car and we had a caravan by the seaside. If she was feeling miserable I'd say, "Would you like some fish and chips?" and off we'd go somewhere for a treat.'

What is the outlook?

Most people who survive a stroke recover their abilities at least to some degree. Much depends on the age and health of the person and on how severe the brain damage was. Determination and will power are important, too.

Stroke patients need well-planned, careful and skilled care from an early stage to achieve maximum recovery, and it may be easier to arrange this in hospital. Rest is not the best thing, because older people quickly lose muscle bulk and strength. A physiotherapist can advise about exercises to get someone moving again and a speech therapist will help if speech has been affected. It is important to start exercising as soon as possible so that stiffness and loss of movement do not set in and become permanent.

For more information, see *Caring for someone who has had a stroke* by Philip Coyne with Penny Mares, published by Age Concern and/or contact The Stroke Association (details on page 256).

Cancer

Cancer is by no means the dreaded incurable disease it was once. But it can develop over a long period of time with very few symptoms, so the diagnosis can then be quite a shock. Each person has to find their own way of coping with what is probably one of the most frightening and lonely situations that they have ever faced. Sometimes it is left to the carer to decide whether the person who is ill should be told. There is also the issue of who else should be told and how.

Case study

Peggy's husband, Bill, went to the doctor with a slight irritating cough that had been bothering him for a while. The doctor sent him to hospital for an X-ray and within four days the family were told that he had lung cancer.

'They told us he had a tumour the size of a grapefruit on his left lung. I was devastated. Bill put his arm round me and said, "We've been together for 45 years and we'll get through this." Really it was him that gave me strength.

'We were referred to the hospital and after that everything seemed to happen very quickly. They took away his whole lung and some of the surrounding tissues. He had the operation on his 70th birthday!

'They kept him in a couple of weeks, and when he was allowed home the district nurse came in every day to change his dressing. It was a huge cut but it healed very well. Gradually he picked up and we carried on. He couldn't play golf any more because he couldn't swing the golf club but he still went round the course with his friends and he still went fishing. We went on holiday as usual in the July.'

Like Bill, many people get a cancer diagnosis from a doctor when they are feeling quite healthy or only a little under the weather. People vary in how they react to this kind of crisis. They vary in how long they need to absorb the information and how much they can take in at a time. But there is often a pattern to these reactions, which is rather like the patterns associated with bereavement. In a way, a diagnosis of a serious condition is like a bereavement:

- Shock and disbelief may come first – I can't believe this is happening to me.
- Denial – they must have made a mistake; I need a second opinion.
- Anger and grief – anger may be directed at the doctor; a sense of grief for what is being lost.
- Fear – most people are afraid of illness and of dying.

The diagnosis of a serious condition can leave you feeling powerless because it is something outside your control. Both you as carer and the person who is ill need someone who is prepared to listen and talk about the illness and its consequences. Dr Rob Buckman in his book *I Don't Know What to Say* suggests some ways you can help the person who is ill:

- Accept the feelings and encourage the person to talk about them. You may find it hard to know what to say – most people do – but just showing that you want to listen and understand is a way of giving support.
- Be prepared to listen to the same issues over and over again.
- Be prepared for sharp swings in mood and outlook. This is part of the process of coming to terms with what is happening.
- Recognise your own feelings and try to sort out those that are helpful from those that are not.
- Try to be open and honest about your own feelings.
- If you find it difficult to be open and honest with each other, encourage the person to find someone else to talk to – a friend, another member of the family, the doctor or the nurse.
- Encourage the person to draw on the strength of past experiences. How have difficult situations been coped with in the past?
- Work out gradually how you can be of most help. Avoid the temptation to rush in and take over.
- Let the person take the lead and make decisions about the future and the need for support.
- Your being there may be more important than doing things. Rushing around may make you feel better but maybe your company is more important.
- Get more information so that you can answer general questions about the condition when they are asked.

It isn't possible to provide good information about the possible signs of cancer because they are so variable. But it is sensible to seek medical advice if there are any changes to the way your body normally functions. For more information about cancer, contact Cancerline or Cancer BACUP, both of which provide support and information.

Falls

Older people are particularly at risk of accidents and injuries at home, especially falls. It is estimated that almost a third of people aged over 70 will have at least one fall at home in a year. Usually falls just cause bruising and superficial cuts, though even those can create problems. But the greatest risk from falls is fractures, particularly of the forearm and hip. Hip fractures are more serious because they can affect a person's mobility and thus their ability to live independently. 'Crush' fractures of the vertebrae (backbone) are a cause of severe back pain, disability and deformity. After the menopause many women develop osteoporosis – loss of density in the bones – and are more prone to fractures. Some men can also develop the same condition.

Living with pain

Pain may be acute or chronic:

- Acute pain – sharp, sudden pain – is part of the body's alarm system which signals that something is wrong. You may be in danger of injuring yourself or perhaps you have already injured yourself and that part of your body needs to be rested.
- Chronic pain – pain that may come on gradually and stay with you a long time – serves no such purpose and may cause disability and distress to sufferers and their families.

Fear can make pain worse and many people are afraid of pain. Many conditions that people think are sure to cause pain in fact do not. For example, one in four people with terminal cancer feel no pain at all. It is not always possible to diagnose the cause of chronic pain but most symptoms are treatable in some way. Reassurance is very important and a doctor or nurse should be able to explain how likely it is that the condition will be painful and how that pain can be treated. There is a range of different drug treatments available, from over-the-counter medicines such as paracetamol to stronger pain-killers such as those related to morphine. Sometimes people worry about becoming addicted to morphine but those fears are really unnecessary. Macmillan nurses specialise in pain relief, especially for terminal conditions. Hospice doctors are also very experienced in pain control and can work alongside your GP to provide pain relief for someone being cared for at home.

There are treatments other than drugs which can relieve pain – for example, acupuncture, hypnotherapy, aromatherapy and relaxation techniques. The TENS machine (transcutaneous electrical nerve stimulation) can also be a useful tool. It is a small box that gives out little pulses of electrical energy through pads placed over the painful area. The effect of the electrical pulses on your skin is very similar to a massage. The stimulus causes your body to release its own, natural 'feel good' substances, called endorphins.

Crises in diabetes

When you are caring for someone with diabetes, you need to know what to do if something goes seriously wrong with their blood sugar levels. Diabetes is usually controlled either by diet alone or with tablets or injections of insulin, depending on which type of diabetes it is. Getting exactly the right balance between food, exercise and insulin or tablets isn't easy. However well someone controls their diabetes, there will always be times when their blood sugar goes too high or too low.

- *Hypo*glycaemia is when the blood sugar goes too low.
- *Hyper*glycaemia is when the blood sugar goes too high.

Let's look at each of these situations in turn.

Hypoglycaemia

Case study

Clive said:

'The first time it was terrible. They hadn't warned me that it can make you wet yourself or mess yourself. If you fall over in the street, people assume you are drunk and they ignore you. But now I know if I need to eat. I feel very low – it's like a clock that's beginning to wind down. I get speckles in front of my eyes and I begin to feel cold and clammy. When that happens I just have something sweet – I usually carry glucose tablets in my pocket.'

As Clive says, having a 'hypo', as it's sometimes called, can be extremely unpleasant and if the person falls they can hurt themselves. But it is not usually dangerous in itself as long as someone recognises the signs and knows what to do.

The warning signs

The signs that someone with diabetes has low blood sugar include:

- tingling around the mouth;
- trembling;
- irregular heartbeat;
- blurred vision;
- headache;
- turning very pale;
- feeling faint or weak;
- feeling hungry;
- feeling irritable or grumpy;
- confusion;
- slurred speech;
- strange behaviour;
- unsteadiness;
- poor co-ordination and concentration.

As the body tries to correct the low blood sugar it may release a hormone called adrenaline. This in turn causes:

- sweating;
- rapid heartbeat;
- feelings of anxiety or panic.

If the symptoms go on and the person does not take preventive action, they may become unconscious or even have a fit or more dangerous and alarming symptoms. However, people with diabetes usually become good at recognising the signs themselves and doing something about it. On the other hand, sometimes they get confused or irritable and refuse to take anything.

What to do

Give the person the simplest short-acting carbohydrate available as an instant cure for all the above symptoms:

- a glass of fruit juice;
- glucose tablets or Hypostop gel;
- a sweet sugary drink (not a 'diet' or 'light' drink);
- jam or honey;
- sweets or chocolate (may take longer to act).

Glucose tablets or gel are fast acting and you can buy them from a chemist/pharmacist shop. Make sure there are some around the house and that the person you care for carries some with them whenever they are out.

If the person is unconscious or has a fit:

- Call an ambulance and tell the emergency service that the person has diabetes and is unconscious.
- Place them in the recovery position (see Figure 3 on page 58) on their side with their head tilted back so that the tongue does not block the throat.
- Don't try to make them eat or drink.
- Don't try to get them up.
- Stay with them until help arrives.

Remember that most people recover quite naturally from a 'hypo' even if you don't do anything. Their body will slowly respond by naturally increasing blood sugar levels and they will become conscious again. This process can be speeded up by giving an injection of glucagon, which is a natural hormone that releases sugar from the liver. If you can keep a supply of this in the house and know how to use it, an ambulance may not be necessary.

Case study

Keith said:

'The first time I saw Val having a "hypo" I didn't know what was happening and I was terrified. She blacked out and fell on the floor and all her limbs were jumping about like an epileptic fit. I panicked. I didn't know what to do so I rushed into the kitchen for the sugar jar, but I couldn't find it so I called the doctor.

'Now I'm better prepared. We have a glucose gel in the house and I know how to give her a glucagon injection. When she comes round, I give her little sips of water so she doesn't get dehydrated if she's been sick.

'I think it's important for carers to see someone going into a 'hypo', to prepare them for what to expect. I let the children see Val, too. Although it is upsetting, it's better for them to realise what's happening and what to do about it. They also know that she's going to recover and be perfectly all right afterwards – that's just as important.'

After a 'hypo' the person may feel weak and weepy or they may feel very tired and low.

Case study

Audrey said:

'Coming round from a hypo is the worst. You feel very emotional. You feel you've let yourself down. It makes you aware there is something wrong with you.'

This is when the person needs your time and attention to work through what happened and what might have caused the 'hypo' so that they can try to prevent another happening in the future. The possible causes include:

- taken too much insulin;
- taken too many sulphonylurea tablets or taken them too close together;
- skipped a meal or snack or had a meal later than usual;
- had a meal or snack that didn't include enough carbohydrate;

■ taken more exercise than usual, or some other strenuous activity;

■ drunk alcohol on an empty stomach.

Talking it through can usually pinpoint the cause. If the person has frequent 'hypos', it should be reported to the doctor or nurse.

Hyperglycaemia

When someone with diabetes has too much sugar in their blood it is called hyperglycaemia. Once diabetes is being treated, this is much less common than 'hypos' but can be more serious. It usually happens when someone is feeling ill or has an infection, especially if they stop taking insulin at the same time.

What to look for

Hyperglycaemia usually comes on more slowly than a 'hypo', perhaps at least a day before you notice any signs. The person may be hyperglycaemic if they:

■ feel constantly thirsty;

■ need to pass urine a lot.

These are also symptoms to look out for in someone who has not yet been diagnosed as having diabetes. If either of these happens, contact the doctor or specialist nurse for advice.

The following symptoms may indicate a real emergency. The person with diabetes:

■ feels sick or starts to vomit;

■ feels drowsy;

■ breathes rapidly and shallowly;

■ has flushed, dry skin;

■ seems to be slipping into a coma;

■ has breath that smells of pear drops.

Call an ambulance or take the person to hospital without delay.

Hyperglycaemia is very serious. If someone has these symptoms, they should go to hospital as quickly as possible.

Case study

Clive said:

'When Audrey's diabetes was first diagnosed, her blood sugar was out of control. It was awful. I could hear her moving about upstairs and then there was a crash and she'd fallen down. One day I came back from work and found she'd blacked out. I rang the ambulance but the paramedics couldn't bring her round. They rushed her to hospital and put her on an insulin drip.

'People get the symptoms but they don't know what they mean. They drink a lot and pee a lot – they don't realise it's a classic sign of high blood glucose.'

Key points

■ Your first reaction may well be one of panic but try to remain calm. It will help you to think more clearly.

■ In some kinds of crisis it is sensible to take a while to think through the options before making any decisions.

■ An Advance Directive provides information about how someone wants to be treated in certain circumstances in the future.

■ It is important to plan ahead so that you know whom you can call on to help in a crisis.

■ First aid is the initial treatment given after an accident or when someone has been taken ill unexpectedly. It can improve someone's chances of recovery and sometimes saves lives.

■ It may be impossible to take away all risk without forfeiting the person's own dignity and independence. The level of acceptable risk may become an issue that family members disagree about.

■ A heart attack or a stroke, or unconsciousness in diabetes, is a serious medical emergency, so never delay in calling an ambulance.

4 Financial and legal aspects

Being ill or caring for someone usually involves extra expense. It may mean larger heating bills or buying a new bed. It may involve giving up work or paying someone to help with caring. The first part of this chapter outlines the main benefits that may be available and other financial help for carers and people who are being cared for. The second part of the chapter deals with financial help available for getting alterations carried out to the home to make caring easier. The third part of the chapter looks at some of the legal arrangements involved in taking over responsibility for someone's affairs in the later stages of an illness and making a Will or Advance Directive.

What costs do you need to think about?

You as carer and the person you care for may have additional costs from a number of sources, such as:

- moving to more suitable accommodation;
- rearranging the accommodation (eg moving a bedroom downstairs);
- buying new furniture (eg bed, chairs);
- having adaptations to the home (eg changing the bath to a shower, building ramps);
- extra heating;

- additional telephones;
- ways of getting around outside the home (eg using taxis, extra running costs for the car, adapting the car for wheelchair access);
- people to help around the house or with personal care or to enable you to get a good night's sleep and time off from the caring role.

You may be able to get help with some of these costs, and this is one of the things we look at in this chapter. Even after claiming all the benefits to which you are entitled, you may well find yourself living on a much reduced income. In these circumstances you may find it helpful to get advice on budgeting. If you find yourself in debt, the Citizens Advice Bureau provides help on how to manage financially difficult situations. Age Concern publishes guides on managing taxes and savings, your rights to money benefits and how to raise income using your home as capital (see 'Publications from Age Concern' for more details).

Welfare benefits for carers who work

Case study

Annie said:

'Knowing who you can tap into is vital; otherwise, you just stagger around in the dark ... which is what I did ... for ten years ... working full-time and looking after my partner as well. During all that time nobody told me I could have worked part-time and claimed welfare benefits. It would have made so much difference, as I was at my wits' end and in the end I got ill because of it.'

Carers who work may be able to claim certain state benefits. Whether you can claim usually depends on the level of your earnings and savings. Pensions do not usually count as earnings for means-test purposes. The main benefits you should consider include:

- Carers Allowance (previously called Invalid Carer Allowance), with or without Carer Premium;

- Working Tax Credit;
- Income Support for people under 60;
- Pension Credit for people aged 60 or over;
- Housing Benefit and Council Tax Benefit (Rate Rebate in Northern Ireland).

There are other ways of getting help with Council Tax; for example:

- Second Adult Rebate (part of the Council Tax Rebate scheme);
- Discount Scheme;
- Disability Reduction.

There are discounts and rebates for certain households, for properties occupied by someone with a disability and for people on low incomes. For Council Tax purposes, carers may be considered 'invisible' in certain circumstances, and therefore do not have to pay the tax.

In addition to Attendance Allowance and age-related benefits, the person you care for may be eligible for Disability Living Allowance.

The Independent Living (1993) Fund may provide top-up funding to severely disabled people. Applications must be made before the age of 66 (contact details on page 245).

Carers UK can advise you about what you are eligible for and how to apply.

Case study

Annie said:

'Carers UK have been fantastic. When I heard about them it was like finding buried treasure. I feel quite cross with myself really that I struggled for ten years working full-time without any help before I found them. Then one day ... just by chance ... I picked up a leaflet and there was a help line. I was on that phone for hours at first – I just poured my heart out. But they really sorted me out ... all my benefits and everything. I love the magazine telling you what's happening and what's there to help you.'

Welfare benefits for carers who are not in paid work

The only benefit specifically for carers who are not earning more than a certain amount is Carers Allowance. However, you may also be entitled to Income Support, Pension Credit, Housing Benefit and Council Tax Benefit or Rent Rebate.

Case study

Sarah said:

'Because I gave up work voluntarily to look after Mum and then Dad, I wasn't entitled to any benefits like Jobseeker's Allowance. It took me three attempts for each of them before I managed to get any Attendance Allowance so the three of us were just managing on their pensions. I had to take Dad's pension book up to the hospital each week to get him to sign it so that we could get the money; otherwise, we would only have had Mum's pension coming in to cover everything. They eventually agreed to pay Attendance Allowance for Mum two days after she died.'

Attendance Allowance and Disability Living Allowance are two state benefits intended to help with the extra costs of illness or disability. Both are non-taxable and they don't depend on income, savings or National Insurance contributions. Getting Attendance Allowance or Disability Living Allowance doesn't reduce other benefits such as Income Support, Council Tax Benefit or Housing Benefit. In fact, getting either Attendance Allowance or Disability Living Allowance can lead to an increase in those other benefits or even entitlement for the first time. There are special rules for terminally ill people so that they can get benefit immediately, usually without a medical examination. Getting Attendance Allowance or Disability Living Allowance can also mean that a carer can apply for Carers Allowance or get a discount on their Council Tax.

Carers UK's CarersLine can advise you about the criteria and on your entitlements and how to apply.

What happens to my state pension contributions?

If you leave work and claim Carers Allowance, your basic retirement pension should be safe unless you elected to pay the lower 'married woman's stamp' some years ago. If you cannot claim Carers Allowance, you may in some circumstances be able to claim Home Responsibilities Protection for your pension contributions. Check with your benefits adviser on the exact position and what you have to do to protect your state pension.

For information on benefits, call the Benefits Enquiry Line or visit the Department for Work and Pensions website (details on pages 230 and 239).

Help from local authority social services departments

If you and the person you care for need help and advice, the local authority's social services department can tell you about the various organisations that can help. The phone number of your local office will be in the telephone book. If you need help with caring, a social services care manager will arrange to see you both to discuss your needs and wishes and to find out whether you are eligible for a service. Services can be provided both to you as a carer and to the person you care for. Your needs are linked but will be assessed separately. You may have to pay for any services you receive but the amount will depend on how much you can afford and the cost of the services. Local authority charges for home care should be written down so that you can take the information away with you to read and think about.

Preparing for a carer's assessment

A carer's assessment will look at:

- the kind of help the person you care for needs;
- the help you are giving;
- the services that could be provided.

The social services care manager will ask questions about your caring responsibilities, such as how many hours you spend caring for the person. They will ask questions about your own well-being, such as whether you get enough sleep and whether anyone else helps as another carer.

Before the assessment, it is a good idea to make a full list of everything you do to help look after the person you are caring for. For example:

- cooking for the person you are caring for;
- bathing them;
- helping them to get dressed and/or go to bed at night;
- shopping or going to the shops with them;
- collecting their pension or other benefits;
- helping them go up and down stairs.

The list will form a starting point for discussion. Have a copy of the list ready when the care manager comes. Each carer's needs are different, so it is important to discuss yours in detail with them.

Direct Payments

In most cases, care needs are assessed by a social services care manager who then purchases services on your behalf. A Direct Payment is money given by the social services department to someone, over the age of 16, who needs care or their carer. In England, Wales and Northern Ireland, the money is for you, and the person you care for, to buy the services you need instead of social services buying it on your behalf. Direct Payments must be spent to buy the support you have been assessed as needing. They cannot be used to buy food or clothing. In Scotland, Direct Payment is given *only* to the disabled person; the carer can handle the payment but cannot receive the service.

Case study

John said:

'Before Direct Payments came in we had to have the agency staff that social services had a contract with, and some of them were awful ... untrained and unreliable. We had lots of missed visits ... I remember over a two-week period one Christmas we had fifteen missed visits because they just didn't have the staff to cover. Sometimes only one would come when we needed two to lift Dad ... hopeless, really. Round here there was no choice of agency, either. In each area social services have a contract with only one agency and they won't cross each other's boundaries even if you pay them direct.

'Direct Payments have been marvellous ... they've made all the difference. In this area there's an agency that provides advice to people who get Direct Payments. That's very good because you need a lot of help with some things, like recruitment if you haven't done it before ... there's lots of things you have to think of. We tried getting people through an employment agency to start with but they charge a fee on top of what you pay the carer and that worked out too expensive so we employ direct now. For Dad we got two carers with the Direct Payments and they were much better than the agency staff. They were better trained and much more reliable. We didn't have any missed visits with them, either. There are some problems you have to think about, though ... they need time off, for one thing, and we need help seven days a week. The problem for them, too, is that we need one hour in the morning and half an hour in the evening, so we can't give them a full-time job.

'When Mum started to get ill as well, we got Direct Payments for her too, and they let us make up a package to cover both of them. She's got dementia and needs 24-hour care, so there were economies of scale there. My assessment as a carer gave me six hours a week of Direct Payments to pay for services to meet my needs on top of that ... I think it comes from the Carers Grant to local councils and it's used for respite. Then when Dad died, it got more difficult again because they tried to take some of those hours away but I argued to keep them.

'Now we've live-in carers who I get through a community website for Australians and New Zealanders who are in the UK with a working holiday visa. You pay to put up an advert and I always get lots of replies. My experience with them has always been good … some are very well qualified – nurses and so on. They usually stay only a month or two … they're on a round the world trip or something like that … but they've been very good for us and not expensive at all.'

You don't have to have a Direct Payment if you don't want to. If you prefer it, the social services department can continue to purchase support on your behalf. You can also change your mind about receiving Direct Payments. If you try it and find it is not working out the way you hoped, discuss the problems with your social services care manager. They will see if they can help you to continue but, if not, Direct Payments can be stopped if that is what you prefer. Social services would then resume purchasing services on your behalf.

You can request Direct Payment, as carer, by contacting your social services department and requesting a carer's assessment. Remember that you can have an assessment even if the person you are caring for refuses help.

The National Centre for Independent Living provides advice on independent living and Direct Payments (contact details on page 249).

Getting help with housing repairs

The person you are caring for may be able to get a grant from the local authority to help with the cost of repairing, improving or adapting their home. If the person you care for is living with you, you may be able to get a grant for your own home. Grants do not necessarily cover the full cost of the work done. The arrangements for housing grants in England

and Wales are different from those in Northern Ireland and Scotland. For details contact:

■ a Citizens Advice Bureau;
■ a disability organisation;
■ a local Age Concern;
■ a carer's project;
■ the local authority housing department or social services;
■ Carers UK's CarersLine.

A home improvement agency can give you specific help and advice on applying for a grant, including:

■ identifying what work needs to be carried out;
■ completing the application form;
■ choosing a good builder;
■ ensuring that work is carried out properly.

You can find out whether there is a home improvement agency in your area by getting in touch with the following:

■ England: Foundations;
■ Northern Ireland: Fold Housing Association;
■ Scotland: Care and Repair Scotland;
■ Wales: Care and Repair Cymru.

Their contact details are in the 'Useful addresses' section.

In England and Wales there are three different types of grant:

■ renovation grants;
■ disabled facilities grants;
■ home repair assistance.

What you have to do to apply is the same for all three kinds of grant. They are available to both home owners and private tenants.

Renovation grants

Renovation grants are for large-scale repairs, improvements and adaptations. Grants are awarded on the basis of the owner or tenant's income

85

and savings, and there are other eligibility criteria as well. A grant may have to be repaid if the property is sold by the grant applicant within five years of receiving the grant, but not normally if the applicant dies within that time.

What can you get a grant for?

A renovation grant can be awarded for the following:

- to bring a property up to the legal standard for human habitation;
- to bring a property up to a standard of reasonable repair;
- to provide thermal insulation;
- to provide facilities for space heating;
- to improve the internal arrangements within the property;
- to provide a fire escape or other fire precautions;
- to improve the construction or physical condition of a property;
- to improve the services or amenities within a property;
- to convert an existing property.

Disabled facilities grants

These are provided to help make the home more suitable and help a disabled person manage more independently. People who are registered or registerable as disabled or their carers can apply but there are eligibility criteria. Grants are awarded on the basis of a person's income and savings, and there is a maximum. Work must not start before the grant has been awarded. The council/local authority should ask social services to arrange for an occupational therapist to visit you and make an assessment of needs.

What can you get a grant for?

A disabled facilities grant can be:

- either mandatory, which means that the local authority must award a grant if the person qualifies;
- or discretionary, which means that the local authority can decide whether or not to award a grant according to priorities, which they should publish.

You can get a **mandatory disabled facilities grant** for:

- improving access in and out of the property;
- making the property safe for the disabled person and others who live there;
- improving access to a room used or usable as the principal family room;
- facilitating preparation or cooking of food by the disabled occupant;
- improving access to or providing a room used or usable for sleeping in;
- improving access to or providing a bathroom or toilet;
- improving access and movement around the home to enable the disabled person to care for someone dependent on them who also lives there;
- improving the use of a source of power, light or heat.

There is a maximum amount but, if the work costs more, the local authority may pay the extra as a discretionary grant. Payment of a mandatory grant can be delayed for up to 12 months from the date of the application.

Discretionary disabled facilities grants are awarded to make a property more suitable for the accommodation, welfare or employment of the disabled person.

Equipment and minor adaptations

Local authorities have a duty to provide any additional facilities that they consider to be necessary for the greater comfort and convenience of the disabled person. This might include equipment and minor adaptations such as handrails, grab rails and ramps. This kind of help might be available without applying for a disabled facilities grant or if an application for such a grant is refused. An occupational therapist should be able to provide you with more information.

Home repair assistance

Discretionary home repair assistance is available for small but essential repairs, improvements or adaptations of any kind. Again there are eligibility criteria, which vary from one local authority to another.

How to apply for a grant

Ask your local authority housing department or environmental health department for further information and an application form. Carers UK has booklets giving advice about grants of this type. Call CarersLine for a free copy.

If you are not happy either with the service you have received from the local authority or with the decision made on your application, you can complain in writing to the local authority in the first instance. If you are still not satisfied, you can complain to the Local Government Ombudsman (contact details on page 246).

Managing other people's money

If the person you are caring for can't manage their own money, you might need to do this for them. Depending on the situation, this might range from picking up their pension to selling a property on their behalf.

Case study

John said:

'You need to think ahead to get your finances sorted out to face means-testing. Transferring funds can be done if you think ahead far enough.

'Getting an Enduring Power of Attorney sorted out for both my parents was vital. Fortunately they had both signed the forms in time – while they were able to give consent. I would advise anyone to do that ... it's very useful to have it there when you need it.'

The two main areas you are most likely to need to get involved in if you are caring for someone are:

■ claiming or collecting their pension and other benefits;
■ dealing with their bank and building society accounts.

Collecting a pension and other benefits

If the person you are caring for is temporarily unable to collect their benefits with the system of order books and giros, they can fill in the back of the giro or order slip with your name and sign it. If you have to do this all the time, you need to become their 'agent'. You are then allowed to cash the giro or order on their behalf. Alternatively, most benefits can be paid straight into their bank or building society account.

By April 2005 order books will have been phased out and people are being encouraged to have payment made into a bank, building society or post office account instead. You will need to ask about the system for collecting money on someone else's behalf. There will be a special system set up for people who are not able to use an account but details were not available at the time of writing.

If the person you are caring for can't deal with their own benefits because of mental incapacity, you can apply to act on their behalf. This means that you become their 'appointee'. You are then treated by the Department for Work and Pensions (DWP) as though you were the person claiming benefit, filling in their forms, dealing with their correspondence and receiving their money. This is a big responsibility and someone from the DWP will probably visit you to make sure everything is as it should be.

A Helping Hand for Benefits (GL21) is available from your local office of the Department for Work and Pensions. Carers UK can also help.

Banks and building societies

If the person you are caring for simply wants you to operate a bank or building society account on their behalf, you can take out a third party mandate. A letter to a bank or building society is usually all that is needed. Some banks and building societies have a standard form for this purpose. Alternatively, you can change the account to a joint account so that you can withdraw from the account on their behalf whenever you need to.

Power of Attorney

If the person you are caring for has very complicated financial affairs – for example, several accounts and sources of income – you might consider taking out a Power of Attorney. This is a legal document giving someone control of another person's affairs. The person you are caring for might want to give you power of attorney if they are:

■ physically incapable of managing their affairs, eg they have been paralysed by a stroke;
■ in hospital or nursing home;
■ away on holiday for some time.

To find out more about Power of Attorney, contact:

■ a Citizens Advice Bureau;
■ a law centre;
■ the Public Guardianship office;
■ a solicitor.

A person can only make a Power of Attorney if they know what they are doing, and it lasts only as long as they are mentally capable.

Enduring Power of Attorney

An ordinary Power of Attorney becomes invalid if the person (the 'donor') becomes mentally incapable. An Enduring Power of Attorney remains valid even if the person later becomes mentally incapable but it must be created by someone who is mentally capable at the time. As in John's case (see page 88), his parents had both set up an Enduring Power of Attorney so that he was able to manage their affairs for them when first his father was paralysed following a stroke and then his mother developed Alzheimer's disease.

Obviously all of this needs to be talked through carefully, as the person you care for may not like the idea of giving you unlimited powers. They may also not be able to face the fact that they might become mentally incapable at some point. In the event that you decide to go ahead, you should both get legal advice from one of the agencies listed above. However, it is not essential to pay a solicitor either for advice or to set up the legal documentation. The forms for Enduring Power of Attorney are available to buy over the counter from law stationers.

Court of Protection and Public Guardianship Office

The Court of Protection and the Public Guardianship Office (PGO) look after the financial affairs and property of someone in England and Wales who is mentally incapable of doing this for themselves. (In Northern Ireland this function belongs with the Office of Care and Protection. The system in Scotland is much more complicated and expensive, so take advice.) The PGO appoints a receiver to collect the person's income, pay their bills and generally look after their affairs in their best interests. The receiver can be a relative or a professional person (eg a solicitor) or local authority employee. If you want to apply to become a receiver, the PGO will send you the forms and help you to make your application. There is no need to pay a solicitor to do this.

When you become a receiver, the Court of Protection and the PGO continue to keep an eye on your activities by requiring annual accounts and the payment of an annual fee. You can get further information about becoming a receiver from one of the agencies listed above or by writing to the PGO.

Making a Will

It is very important that all of us make a Will setting out what we want to happen to our property when we die. This applies to you as carer as well as the person you are caring for. Some people find it satisfying to set their affairs in order, knowing that things have been dealt with in the way they want. Others want things sorted out but prefer to delegate the details to other people. For some people the whole idea of dying is too painful to think about. If you both make a Will, this may help to make the process less painful.

The Will names one or more people to be the executors: they are responsible for sorting out the person's money and property and carrying out the instructions in the Will. The executor can either be a close relative or a professional (eg solicitor or bank manager). A professional normally charges a fee, which comes out of the estate.

It is often best to ask a solicitor to help draw up a Will if your affairs are at all complicated. Fees vary widely, so it is worth while ringing round solicitors to find out what they would charge. Some people draw up their own Will, and pre-printed documentation is available (with guidance on how to complete it), either from a good stationer or from the Consumers' Association; Age Concern has a helpful Factsheet, *Making your Will*. The Will must be signed, dated and witnessed in the right way to be valid. The executor can be a beneficiary but the witnesses to the signature and their relatives may not.

See Chapter 8 for what to do when someone dies.

Advance Directives and Living Wills

In Chapter 3 Malcolm and Penny explained how their daughter Paula had written an Advance Directive about her mental health care, which doctors and nurses could use in a crisis.

Although it is not legally binding, an Advance Directive is a way of recording what someone would like to happen about their future in terms of:

■ care
■ medical treatment
■ financial affairs

You can use an Advance Directive, for example, to set out your wishes about who should manage your financial affairs as a receiver if you become incapable of managing them yourself or unable to express your views.

A Living Will is a type of Advance Directive that includes information about the circumstances under which someone would like to accept or refuse medical treatment. Doctors are not bound to follow all your wishes, so it is a good idea to discuss your views with them and give them a copy of the document. On the other hand, in England and Wales, an Advance Directive that refuses treatment to prolong life is legally binding on doctors, provided it is clear that the person was fully mentally capable when they made the decision. Not everyone likes the idea of a written document. Some people prefer simply to discuss their wishes confidentially with someone they are close to and to entrust this person with making their views known at the appropriate time.

Other practical arrangements

There is a whole range of financial and legal matters to take into account when you are caring for someone. We have looked at some of them in this chapter but there may be other considerations, such as:

- Giving up work or changing to part-time work.
- Making arrangements for the future of children under 18; for example, appointing guardians if both parents should die.
- Making a list of important documents and where they are kept; for example, Will, marriage certificate, title deeds of the house, bank and building society accounts, insurance policies, pension schemes.
- Making a list of people who should be informed in the event of death; for example, solicitor, executors named in the Will.
- Leaving a body for medical research or organ donation – a GP will be able to advise on this. Age Concern Factsheet 27 *Planning for a funeral* explains the procedure.
- Any wishes for the funeral service, burial or cremation, and any gathering after the funeral.
- Pre-paid funeral plans – the British Institute of Funeral Directors (contact details on page 232) can send you a leaflet explaining how to arrange and pay for a funeral in advance.
- Reducing Inheritance Tax – see *Your Taxes and Savings* published annually by Age Concern.

Key points

■ Being ill or caring for someone usually involves extra expense.

■ If you need help with budgeting or if you find yourself in debt, the Citizens Advice Bureau provides help on how to manage financially difficult situations.

■ Age Concern publishes guides on managing taxes and savings, your rights to money benefits and how to raise income using your home as capital.

■ Carers UK provides advice on welfare benefits, your rights as a carer, eligibility and entitlements, and how to apply.

■ If you and the person you care for are eligible for services from your local authority social services department, you may have to pay for any services you receive but the amount will depend on how much you can afford and the cost of the services.

■ A Direct Payment is given by social services to someone, over the age of 16, who needs care or (in England, Wales and Northern Ireland) their carer, to buy the services you need instead of a care manager buying it on your behalf. In Scotland this is given *only* to the disabled person, although the carer can handle the payment.

■ If the person you are caring for can't deal with their own benefits because of mental incapacity, you can apply to act on their behalf.

■ If the person you are caring for wants you to operate a bank or building society account on their behalf, you can take out a third party mandate.

■ A person can make a Power of Attorney only if they know what they are doing, and it lasts only as long as they are mentally capable.

■ An Enduring Power of Attorney remains valid even if the person later becomes mentally incapable but it must be created by someone who is mentally capable at the time.

(Continued)

■ It is very important that all of us make a Will setting out what we want to happen to our property when we die. This applies to you as carer as well as the person you are caring for.

■ An Advance Directive is a way of recording what someone would like to happen about their future in terms of their care, medical treatment and financial affairs.

■ A Living Will is a form of Advance Directive that sets out the person's wishes regarding treatment if they become extremely ill, to the point where they are unable to speak for themselves; for example, the instruction 'do not resuscitate' if they have a severe stroke as well.

■ The person you are caring for may be able to get a grant to help with the cost of repairing, improving or adapting their home. If the person you care for is living with you, you may be able to get a grant for your own home.

5 Dealing with the health and social care system

Sometimes finding the right help isn't easy, and you may get angry and frustrated with the red tape and delays. This chapter explains who the people are in the health and social care systems, what they do and how to find your way around. We also look at how best to work with health and social care professionals, including making a complaint.

We do not deal with welfare benefits in this chapter, because they are administered by local offices of the Department for Work and Pensions. This is a central government department, which is separate and different from local authority social services departments.

Every NHS Trust should have or be developing a Patient Advice and Liaison Service (PALS). PALS should provide support and information to patients, carers and families about local health services.

NHS Direct is a telephone advice and information service, available throughout England and Wales (Scotland has NHS24), staffed by experienced nurses. It provides advice and information about health, illnesses and health services. NHS Direct also has an online website that gives information about health services, treatment choices, medical conditions and self-help groups. Touch-screen terminals are being provided in supermarkets and pharmacies so that people who are not connected to the internet can use the service there. (Telephone and website details are given on page 249.)

Let's begin by looking at the structures of the health and social services.

Local authority social services

Your first point of contact with the social care system is likely to be with a social services care manager, who will assess your needs as a carer and the social care needs of the person you care for. A decision will then be made as to your eligibility for a service, depending on the local authority's eligibility criteria, before agreeing with you and the person you care for what services will be provided. Social services staff will often be able to advise you on the welfare benefits that you might qualify for, but they have no control over benefits budgets or decisions made by staff at the Department for Work and Pensions. On the other hand, services provided via the local authority are sometimes charged for and a social services care manager may have to make a financial assessment of your ability to pay those charges. This process is discussed in Chapters 4 and 6. Direct payments are discussed in Chapter 4.

The kinds of services that local authorities might fund include:

- Domiciliary care – care workers visiting your home to provide personal care.
- Small adaptations to your home such as grab rails and bath seats.
- Respite care so that you can have a break.
- Residential care.
- Day centres.
- Volunteer drivers.
- Carers' support groups.
- Counselling.
- Therapy services for people with mental health problems.

Primary health care

Your first point of contact with the health care system was probably registering with your GP. Primary health services are provided by GPs and the other staff, such as practice nurses, who work in or from local GP surgeries. Other primary care professionals include dentists, pharmacists, chiropodists and optometrists. It is primary health care professionals who offer most health care support to carers.

GP practices in each area are managed by Primary Care Trusts (PCTs). PCTs hold the NHS budget for all the health care of the population they serve. A large part of this money is used to make sure that hospital care and other specialist treatment is available. Each PCT is responsible for identifying which health care services the local population needs and ensuring that they are provided. It does this by providing some services itself and commissioning all other health care services on behalf of the patients registered with it. This includes secondary health care – for example, hospital treatment and rehabilitation. It also includes mental health and learning disability services.

Family doctor and community health services

The family doctor (general practitioner, GP) provides primary care and acts as the gatekeeper to health care services. Your GP should be able to put you in touch with community health services. If necessary, arrangements can usually be made for you to be seen at home. The kinds of people who may help, or services that might be available, include:

■ district nurse or community nurse – carries out nursing procedures such as changing dressings;
■ chiropodist – provides foot care;
■ continence adviser – provides practical equipment such as continence pads and advice on how to manage continence;

- physiotherapist – gives structured exercise to promote rehabilitation and mobility;
- community psychiatric nurse – supports people with mental health problems;
- hospice at home or Macmillan nurse – provides care for people who are terminally ill;
- occupational therapist – advises on how to adapt your home to make care easier.

GP appointments

Surgeries work to very tight schedules – the average GP appointment lasts only six minutes. If you show you understand how they work and are a responsible patient, they are more likely to be sympathetic to your needs. Appointment systems vary from one surgery to another but, if you can, try to book appointments for follow-up well in advance. If you need extra time, ask for a double appointment. If it is difficult for you or the person you care for to wait in the surgery, try asking for the first appointment of the session. If you have to miss an appointment, be sure to ring the surgery and let them know so that someone else can use the time.

If you use the same GP practice as the person you care for, make separate appointments to discuss your own health. Ask your GP to make a note of your caring role on your medical notes. This should help to ensure you are given special consideration (eg for home visits). If you feel your own health is suffering because of the work you do as a carer, ask for help.

When your GP surgery is closed, there is normally an out-of-hours service. You can telephone it if there is a medical problem that cannot wait until the next working day. If you are unsure what to do, ring NHS Direct (NHS24 in Scotland) for advice. There are normally also out-of-hours arrangements for pharmacies, too; these should be published in the local newspaper.

Home visits for the general public are much less common than they used to be. However, if the person you care for is housebound, you should not have to take them to the surgery for an appointment. Community nurses carry out home visits – to change dressings, for example. They may also be able to give or arrange for practical help such as showing you how to give injections or to move the person you care for from one place to another without damaging yourself (see Chapter 2). Repeat prescriptions can sometimes be delivered to your home if it is difficult for you to get to the surgery; some pharmacists can arrange to collect prescriptions from the surgery. Some dentists and other health care workers also make home visits. You can ask them if they provide this service and, if not, where it is available. The local PALS service should have this information, too.

Whoever you are dealing with, if you have a lot of questions, write them down to remind yourself. It can also help to make a note of the answers so that you can look at them again when you are more relaxed. If the person you speak to first doesn't provide you with the information you need, try someone else. Receptionists and practice managers often keep a lot of information and leaflets behind the desk not on general display. Local pharmacists should be able to provide information about prescribed drugs and their side-effects. They can also tell you whether you need to see a doctor. NHS Direct is a good source of general information and advice. (See also Chapter 7.)

Confidentiality

There may be times when it is necessary for you to see a health professional on behalf of the person you care for. Doctors and nurses are often reluctant to give information about patients to their carers – every patient has a right to privacy. It will help if the person you care for tells health professionals that they agree to information being given to their carer. If this is not possible, explain to the doctor or nurse why you need the information. It is important that the practice makes a note of your caring role. A doctor should be able to give you enough information about the person you care for to enable you to care safely and with peace of mind. If you have worries, make your concerns clear.

Hospital services

Hospitals, providing specialist and 'acute' (short-term) care, are usually managed separately from Primary Care Trusts. Hospitals offer both in-patient care (eg for surgery) and out-patient clinics where you can see a specialist. Each area usually has a Hospital Trust, which covers all the acute hospitals in that area. Hospital care is described as secondary care. Your GP is the person who will refer you to the hospital for specialist services. The only part of a hospital that you can go to without being referred in this way is the Accident and Emergency department. In some areas there are also community hospitals providing long-term care, called continuing care.

Services for people with mental health problems and learning disabilities, including mental hospitals, are usually provided by a separate Trust. This may be funded and provided jointly by health and social services departments. However, structures vary a great deal from place to place.

Intermediate care

Intermediate care is intended to bridge possible gaps between health and social services. It provides rehabilitation and 'step down' services to people (older people in particular) who have finished their hospital treatment but who are not yet ready to manage independently at home. It may be provided in a care home or in a person's own home and is likely to be limited to a maximum of six weeks (the sort of intermediate care provided varies from one area to another).

The Government has announced a major programme of investment in intermediate care, with the aim of helping more older people maintain independent lives at home. Initial guidance has been issued which defines what intermediate care is and how it links in with other related services. These services are being developed over the next few years and different areas may well develop differently.

To be defined as 'intermediate care' all of the following criteria have to be met. The services must:

- be targeted at people who would otherwise face unnecessarily prolonged hospital stays or inappropriate admission to acute hospital care or long-term care in a care home;
- be provided on the basis of a comprehensive assessment, with a care plan that involves active therapy, treatment or the opportunity for recovery;
- have a planned outcome – typically enabling the person to resume living at home;
- be time-limited, normally no longer than six weeks and often as little as one to two weeks;
- involve health and social care professionals working together.

All care plans should have a review date within six weeks.

Exceptionally, intermediate care can be extended. Although someone may still continue to receive some longer term rehabilitation services or home care following a period of intermediate care, this is separate from intermediate care. Both you and the person you care for should be closely involved in drawing up the care plan.

Intermediate care is varied to suit the person's needs. There could be a range of services such as rapid response teams to allow rapid access to care at home to prevent the person having to go into hospital, together with input from community equipment services or housing support services where necessary. It could involve a 'hospital at home' service, which gives intensive support at home either to avoid hospital admission or to enable early discharge from hospital; it could be more appropriate to have a short-term programme of therapy in a residential setting or a short period of rehabilitation before returning home. Intermediate care might be rehabilitation services provided in a day hospital or day centre.

It is not the Government's intention that people should be charged for care that comes under this definition of 'intermediate care'. Because the aim is to ensure that the services work closely together, it could be either the NHS or social services that takes the lead in providing the care. Normally, social services charge for the care they provide; if the person's care plan indicates that intermediate care is involved, though, there should be no charge. However, if there are charges for home care services already in place, which are not part of the intermediate care package, it might be necessary to continue paying for them.

What are rehabilitation and recovery services?

Rehabilitation covers a variety of services, such as speech therapy (eg to help with speech or swallowing functions), physiotherapy (eg to help with mobility) or occupational therapy (eg to see how aids and adaptations can assist). A period of recovery after acute hospital treatment may also be needed, to include regaining confidence about going back home. Intermediate care is intended to fill this role but is strictly time-limited. In some circumstances, rehabilitation and recovery services might be needed to continue beyond this time limit. Some people need help with regaining life skills after a period of sudden or prolonged illness. This is where occupational therapy can help someone to relearn how to manage their own lives.

Coming out of hospital

Leaving hospital can be a difficult experience, especially if the hospital stay has been a long one. Sometimes the person leaving hospital is unable to function as they did before, either physically or mentally. You might not have really considered yourself a carer until now or might perhaps be trying to adjust to a completely new situation. It can be helpful for you to know more about hospital discharge planning.

When someone is discharged from hospital, it means that the doctor in charge of their care is satisfied that they are well enough to leave, provided they have the support or help they need at home. What happens to them after they leave hospital – where they go and what help they get (if any) – should be planned while they are still in hospital as part of hospital discharge planning. A hospital discharge plan should include:

■ The name of a specific member of staff at the hospital who is responsible for checking that the patient is discharged properly.
■ Details of any support, help, equipment or adaptations that are to be set up before discharge and information about who is responsible for their provision.
■ Details of any contacts to be made to the primary and community health services; eg GP, district nurse, social services care manager.

Hospitals are meant to take special care when discharging patients who:

■ live alone;
■ are frail or elderly;
■ live with an elderly carer;
■ have a serious illness or a continuing disability;
■ have a mental illness;
■ are in need of special help (eg with continence);
■ have communication difficulties (eg following a stroke);
■ are terminally ill.

They should also take carers' needs into account. Leaving hospital can be traumatic, especially if the person you care for has been in hospital for a long time or has been seriously ill. Maybe this is the point at which you are taking on the role of carer for the first time.

What the hospital should do

There are a number of things the hospital staff should do on the day itself to make sure that a patient is discharged properly and everything goes smoothly. You might like to use the following checklist to make sure the person you care for is discharged properly:

- Has at least 24 hours' notice been given before discharge?
- Has transport home been arranged if necessary?
- Have any property and valuables been returned to the patient?
- Have any essential equipment, training or fittings been supplied?
- Has the patient's GP been told that they are being discharged?
- Have any necessary medicines been supplied?
- Have you both been provided with information about any symptoms to watch out for?
- Do you both know where to get help if needed?

What you can do

You or other members of the family or friends can also help the day go smoothly by:

- Bringing in any outdoor clothes required – maybe the weather is warmer or colder than when the patient was admitted.
- Providing or arranging transport if this is not being organised by the hospital.
- Making sure the person's home is in order if they are going home – temperature, food to eat, cleanliness.
- Making sure there are no new safety issues to deal with – if the person is on crutches, what about the flooring?

If the patient is going home alone, is there someone to go with them and stay for a few hours or days if necessary? In some areas there are voluntary organisations that have 'home from hospital' schemes to provide support during the first few days.

Many hospitals have made great efforts to improve the way they discharge patients but there are still occasions when their procedures aren't up to standard. If you are not happy with the way in which the person you care for is discharged, you can complain.

If there is anything about hospital discharge arrangements that you don't understand, the PALS service may be able to provide further information.

Case study

John said:

'Dad had a stroke in '96 and was hospitalised in Doncaster. I was working in London in the civil service at the time and initially just came up to help Mum. The hospital thought Dad would die and in fact withdrew food and water on that basis ... but he didn't. He got pneumonia and they didn't want to treat him but we insisted that they should and he started to recover. Then we persuaded them to put him on a drip ... because he would have been very dehydrated by then; after a month ... he was still alive ... with a bit more persuading, they started feeding him through a stomach tube ... but by then of course he'd lost a lot of weight and was very weak. The main hospital didn't want him staying there so they involved social services because they wanted to discharge him. But social services said he was much too ill to send home. After a couple of months they sent him on to a long-term hospital ... but he wasn't in the stroke unit as he was thought too badly affected for rehabilitation and of course he was still very weak because he hadn't been fed.

'Eventually, social services got involved again and started to arrange for him to come home. They had a case conference to talk about how many visits a day he would need from the district nurse and the sort of equipment we needed to look after him. What we didn't realise at the time was that some key people were missing from the case conference ... like the district nurse. And when we got him home she wanted to over-ride the decisions made at the case conference. She made her own decisions about what to do and it wasn't what they'd said. Looking back, I think that was a crucial turning point ... not having all the key people at the case conference.

'Dad was paralysed down one side, had a feeding tube into his stomach and was doubly incontinent. Two carers came in the morning to get him washed and dressed and they came at night to get him back to bed. Someone came at lunchtime, too, because he needed help with feeding. Mum needed help with all the washing and ironing, because the bed was wet every night and she was having difficulty coping. After a bit social services tried to knock the hours down but I argued with them that we needed all that time and Mum wasn't coping well even with the help as I'd gone back to work part-time locally by then. Anyway, they decided that the carers shouldn't do washing and ironing even though that was what we really needed help with and knocked the time down by 15 minutes a day.

'The dentist did home visits once a year for my dad and the optician too. But Dad's GP was really not supportive at all … he never came or asked how things were going … and things just went from bad to worse with the district nurse. His catheter kept getting blocked and infected, and once when I called the district nurse she said she couldn't come till the next day. I said she had to come that day as he was in pain … but that was it … once you fall out with them there's no going back really.

'When it first became obvious that Mum was developing dementia, she used to go to a day centre and the nurse there was really helpful … she came out to visit her at home and helped us get her into a centre that was nearer to home. She can't go now as she just needs too much one-to-one attention – she's not very mobile and has had some nasty falls so it would be too much responsibility for them. But she is entitled to 24-hour care, so that helps.'

John's experience of hospital care for his father and the discharge procedures was not a good one. But he stood up for his parents' rights and managed to achieve a satisfactory outcome particularly with regard to care at home funded by social services. (In Chapter 4 he talked about his good experience of using Direct Payments.)

Age Concern Factsheet 23 *Help with continence*; Factsheet 5 *Dental care and older people*; and Factsheet 20 *NHS continuing care, free nursing care and intermediate care* may be helpful in similar circumstances.

Carers and hospital discharge

The Department of Health issued good practice guidance, called *The Hospital Discharge Workbook*, which is still in use (to obtain a copy, see page 239). Quoting this guidance, the website Carersnet.org.uk said, in its January 2003 Newsletter:

> 'The power and control exhibited by many professions needs to change from one of professional dominance to one where power and control are shared. Professionals bring the professional and technical expertise; patients and carers bring their individual experience, expertise and aspirations.'

A key message of the Department of Health publication is to recognise the important role that carers play and their right to assessment and support. It says that carers must be taken into account in discharge planning and be given a choice about undertaking a caring role. The intention is that there will be ward-based care co-ordinators who will arrange to see carers separately and finalise the arrangements 48 hours before discharge. Consideration of carers' needs should begin at the pre-admission assessment. The guidance also requires consultation with all concerned (sometimes called 'stakeholders'), including carers' organisations, regarding the development of new discharge procedures whereby the health and social services work together.

Case study

Malcolm talked a bit about his role as co-ordinator for his local Rethink branch:

'People who come to us are sometimes very angry because they can't understand what's going on. Some are carers like us and some are service users ... people with a mental illness ... we work with both sides. One of the common problems is that they don't know how the system works ... can't grasp who all the professionals are that they see ... don't know about the medication they've been given ... don't know how to get what they want. So I can explain a bit about the Community Mental Health Trust. We tell people who everyone is … like what a CPN (Community Psychiatric Nurse; now often called a mental health nurse) does or a community support worker. We know a bit about the different kinds of medication and their side-effects because we get lots of information from Rethink. I can also link people into advocacy services or act as a go-between in the relationship between carers and professionals, too.

'Our mental health services have been much better at involving patients and carers than other parts of the NHS. For example, Rethink has been represented for several years now on the Joint Commissioning and Planning Board, which plans local mental health services. I go to those meetings and we do have some success in getting our point of view across. I'm also part of the CPA Task Force … let me explain. The Care Programme Approach (CPA) is a method of care planning that the mental health professionals use now with patients who are mentally ill. It is about assessing care needs and setting up a care package to meet those needs with regular reviews. The Task Force was established to implement this way of working. I think it helps to focus the minds of professionals to have someone like me there putting the carer's point of view. At the same time it has helped me to understand their perspective. Professionals sometimes suffer from the same sort of frustrations that I do because they haven't the time and money to run the services in the way they would really like to. When things go wrong, the temptation is to get angry and blame the professionals and leave them to sort it out by themselves. But it's much more productive to try to work together to find a way out of it. I think both sides benefit from involving patients and carers.'

As Malcolm explained, carers' organisations can perform an important function in bringing carers, service users and professionals closer together.

National health and social care structures

The Department of Health sets the policy and targets on health and social care, provides the funding and monitors performance. The pattern of health and social care services is not uniform across the country: it differs from one place to another. However, there is a National Service Framework for each group of people – older people, people with mental health problems, etc – and targets for particular health conditions such as cancer and heart disease.

- **CHAI** – the Commission for Healthcare Audit and Inspection monitors the performance of NHS Trusts and independent health care against the Government's targets and makes recommendations for improvement. Their website (see page 236) tells you about their functions and you can read their inspection reports.
- **CSCI** – the Commission for Social Care Inspection regulates (ie registers and inspects) a range of care services provided by the independent and voluntary sector (eg care homes and domiciliary care). It also handles complaints about regulated services so, if you believe there is a serious problem with a regulated service and you have been unable to get the service to address the problem, you should complain to the CSCI. The CSCI also monitors the work of local authority social services departments. The website (see page 236) tells you about its functions and its reports are published.

New developments in joint working

The Government is proposing a number of measures to ensure that health and social services work more closely with each other. These will change the way that help is provided. The most important changes are:

- **Care Trusts** – these are new bodies, which will provide care on behalf of both local Primary Care Trusts and social services departments. They will be set up only where local authorities and health authorities agree that they are the best way to provide services.
- **Partnership Boards** – joint planning bodies for services for people with learning disabilities.

Patient Forums

The NHS Plan (2000) put forward as part of its vision for the future that patients and carers should have more say in the way health care is provided. One of the ways for this to happen is through the establishment of a Patient Forum for each NHS trust in England; these came into being in December 2003. (Wales, Scotland and Northern Ireland have retained Community Health Councils to perform this function.) In January 2003 the Commission for Public, Patient and Community Involvement was established. The Commission appoints volunteer members (and staff) to the Patient Forums.

Part of the role of a Patient Forum is to monitor and review the health care services provided to patients and report back its findings to the NHS trust. However, foundation hospitals that are to be given independent status will not have a Patient Forum.

Key points

■ Remember that you are important. As a caring relative or friend, you are important to their well-being. In fact, your support can be more important than all the other services put together.

■ Remember that you should be offered choices, so don't allow yourself to be pushed into doing something you don't want to do.

■ Be well prepared before you talk to professionals. Make a list of all the points you want to make and questions you want to ask, ticking them off as you go along. Make a note of what they say.

■ Be polite but firm. You may find it helps to have someone with you for moral support. (Sarah suggested: 'My advice is just keep phoning, writing and hassling people to get what you want. They'll give in in the end just to get rid of you.')

■ See the other person's point of view. If you are feeling upset or angry, it can be hard to listen properly to what the other person is saying. Remember that they are human, too. It may help if you are sympathetic to their position. ('I know you are under a lot of pressure …', 'I really appreciate what you have done so far …').

■ Keep names and phone numbers of all the people you deal with and note down what they do (eg job title and role). You may want to put a star against the names of those who were particularly helpful.

■ Keep a record of dates when you spoke to each person and make a note of when they said something would happen. Chase them up if it doesn't happen.

■ Don't be afraid to complain if you are not happy with the way you are being treated. All public services have complaints procedures. Just ring the main number for the service and say you want to make a complaint.

6 Considering longer term care options

Many people find themselves taking on a caring role, perhaps in an emergency, without any opportunity for planning ahead. Maybe you thought caring would only be a short-term arrangement but the problems that brought you into the role have not gone away or are becoming more pressing. Eventually you need to take stock of the situation, consider your current position, consider the options and make plans for the future. These are the things we consider in this chapter.

Looking at the options

The first step is to consider whether it may be possible for the present arrangements to continue – if this is what you would both prefer – by arranging extra services or care at home. Different services are available from health authorities, housing departments and social services departments, depending on where you live. The following may help you to 'test' what is possible or best for your situation.

■ Is there a medical problem? Many people have problems such as incontinence or depression, or perhaps problems with medication that can be identified and helped without the need for any other change. An appropriate specialist (eg a geriatrician, who specialises in the medical problems of older people), might be contacted through your GP to provide advice.

- Is there a problem with the house itself that is making you think of moving? Have you asked your local authority, or any housing associations in your area, about options such as sheltered housing?
- If there is a problem with the bath or toilet or stairs, have you asked the social services department to help with some equipment or adaptations to your home? Or have you asked the housing department about grants for adaptations?
- If the home is in poor repair, could you raise some money to help pay for what you need? Or have you asked your local housing department if there is any help through grants with these costs?
- Have you found out about all the welfare benefits that might help you as carer and the person you care for?

Even if you have arranged quite a lot of support, you may find that there are still problems. If the person you care for lives alone and wants to stay there, you will no doubt be concerned for their welfare. However, remember that many people with care needs live alone very successfully. You could suggest trying it out for a trial period, and keep in touch on a regular basis to see how things are going.

A companion at home

Some people feel that they could manage at home if there were someone else living in their home, perhaps helping with light care tasks, or just 'keeping a watchful eye'. Some people feel their home is too big for one or two but do not wish to move. It is sometimes possible to find a companion, or 'living-in help'. Some local agencies may be able to help, or you might consider advertising in local newspapers, magazines or church journals. If you do advertise for a companion or a helper, it is advisable to use a box number and always to take up references.

You should carefully consider exactly what you want a companion to do. Write this down to form a 'job description' so that there is no misunderstanding by either party as to what is expected. You might like to seek legal advice on whether a contract could be drawn up. The Citizens Advice Bureau can explain responsibilities for National Insurance and other considerations such as health and safety.

The following national publications may prove useful in helping to find a companion:

- *Choice* magazine: published monthly (contact details on page 236).
- National daily newspapers.
- *The Lady*: published Tuesdays; submit advertisements in writing (contact details on page 246).

There are also websites such as the one John talked about in Chapter 4. Whatever the source, be sure to check that the person is reliable and responsible.

Employment agencies, nursing agencies and domiciliary care agencies

There are private agencies that recruit and place living-in companions and daily or longer-term nurses or care workers. Some helpers will not undertake more than light household duties. Heavy washing, ironing and cleaning may have to be done by someone else. Agencies (in England) that provide nurses or care workers who carry out personal care tasks have to register with the Commission for Social Care Inspection (in Wales it is the Care Standards Inspectorate for Wales, CSIW; in Scotland it is the Scottish Commission for the Regulation of Care, SCRC; in Northern Ireland, new regulatory arrangements for agencies are not yet in place). They are regularly inspected by the Commission to make sure that they comply with national minimum standards. These standards include requirements to train staff, provide detailed information about their services and have written contracts with service users.

In order to provide 'permanent' help, many agencies operate a rota system with the paid carers working for a period of one or two weeks or a month, and then changing over in a planned way with another care worker. This ensures continuity, where it may be difficult to find one person to live in permanently. Each agency has its own system for placing staff, and charges and style of service vary considerably. There is usually a weekly agency fee on top of the wage paid to the care worker.

In the past, some employment agencies used a system whereby staff were self-employed and responsible for their own training and tax and National Insurance contributions. However, agencies are now responsible, as employers, for care workers whom they place.

Local agencies are listed in the *Yellow Pages* under 'Employment Agencies and Consultants' or 'Nurses' Agencies and Care Agencies'. The United Kingdom Home Care Association (UKHCA), whose member organisations provide care at home, has a leaflet 'Choosing care in your home'. Single copies are available free from UKHCA (contact details on page 256). The charity Counsel and Care (contact details on page 237) has a database of home care agencies around the UK.

Sheltered housing

There are many types of sheltered accommodation available, either to rent or to buy. Often it is fairly independent and self-contained in three or four rooms with its own front door. Usually, there is a warden on site who keeps an eye on tenants. The warden is not expected to provide nursing or caring, but may arrange for help when needed. Most schemes have alarm systems that tenants can operate in an emergency.

There are some 'very sheltered' or 'extra care' housing schemes (also sometimes called 'assisted housing'), which may be of interest. These have a higher level of support than in ordinary sheltered housing. Sometimes this support can be similar to that in a care home but the difference is that the person is a tenant in what becomes their own home. Other schemes may provide meals, round-the-clock warden cover, and domestic assistance of the type a 'home help' might provide;

or additional help might be arranged or provided by the local authority social services department.

If you are thinking about moving into rented sheltered accommodation, you need to check exactly what services are in place under the terms of the tenancy. Talk to other tenants to find out how good the service is. Similar advice applies if you are planning to buy.

For more information

i See Age Concern Factsheet 8 *Moving into rented housing* and Factsheet 2 *Buying retirement housing*.

i The Elderly Accommodation Counsel (contact details on page 242) also has information about sheltered housing.

Unable to manage at home

If the person you are caring for is unable to continue to live at home or you are unable to continue to care for them, you may need to think about a care home. Here we look at:

■ How you feel about care homes.
■ Finding a care home.
■ Paying for a care home.
■ Making the transition from home to care home.

In the recent past it was possible to make a clear distinction between residential care homes and nursing homes. Now the distinction between care homes is less clear, so you will need to look carefully at the prospectus for each home to find out the kind of care services they provide.

How you feel about care homes

The decision to go into a care home is not easy. It means that the person you care for has to leave their own home and familiar surroundings.

117

However, there could be real benefits to be gained through new care and companionship. The important thing is to make sure that you've both found out what all the possibilities are and then decided what's best.

Going into a care home should be the person's own decision. *No one* can be forced to go into a home against their will except in very exceptional circumstances. These circumstances are explained in Age Concern Factsheet 41 *Local authority assessment for community care services*.

From your point of view as carer, it might be difficult to even think about whether a care home is a possibility. It's easy to feel as though you are rejecting someone or giving up on them. Many carers feel guilty or that they have failed in some way if the person they are caring for goes into a care home. But it's important to remember that you can do only so much as a carer. If the person you are caring for is unable to look after themselves and/or you are unable to provide the care they need – whatever the reason – a care home is a sensible and realistic option. It is better to arrange proper care for someone than to struggle on until you reach crisis point.

It may not be possible to arrange adequate care and support you both need at home. Some situations may now be too difficult or stressful to cope with any longer at home. In an ideal situation, you will be able to talk openly and honestly about this with the person you are caring for. They may accept the situation more readily than you expect. Perhaps they want to be in the same care home as a friend or other people they know. Perhaps they can be near to where you live. The person you care for may positively want some of the advantages that a care home can offer. It may indeed be the best option. If that is the case, you both need to know as much as possible about different care homes to be able to make the right choice.

If the person you are caring for is unwilling or unable to discuss the situation, it may help you to talk it over with someone else who isn't involved. A professional such as your GP or a social worker may be able to help. You may know someone who has been in a similar situation or perhaps a friend will listen and help you sort things out in your own mind. If you have considered all the options and a care home seems to be the best option over all, you should be happy in your mind that you are doing the right thing.

What is a care home?

Since April 2000, all care homes in England have been registered with the National Care Standards Commission (NCSC); in 2004 this was replaced by the Commission for Social Care Inspection (CSCI). In Wales it is the Care Standards Inspectorate for Wales (CSIW); in Scotland it is the Scottish Commission for the Regulation of Care (SCRC); and in Northern Ireland the Department of Education for Northern Ireland (DENI).

A distinction is made between:

■ care homes
■ care homes (nursing).

Nursing care can be provided only by care homes (nursing). Both kinds of care home provide personal care: washing, bathing, dressing and going to the toilet.

If you want information about all the registered care homes in your area, you can get it either from the CSCI or from your local social services department (in Scotland the social work department and in Northern Ireland the Health and Social Services Trust). You can also get help and advice from:

■ Carers UK's CarersLine;
■ a Citizens Advice Bureau;
■ a welfare rights unit;
■ a disability organisation;
■ a local branch of a voluntary organisation;
■ a carers' project.

Care homes in general cater for a wide range of vulnerable people, including older people, people with learning difficulties or those with mental health problems or drug and alcohol problems. But each care home will normally specialise in providing care to people with one particular set of care needs. When looking for a care home, it is important to find one that provides the right kind of care services for the person who is going to live there.

Regulation of care homes

All care homes providing personal care and/or nursing care are required by the Care Standards Act 2000 to register with, and be inspected by, the appropriate national regulatory body. Registration should be granted only in the following circumstances:

- the people owning and running the home are suitable;
- services and facilities meet national minimum standards;
- the building is appropriate.

The certificate of registration specifies the number and type of residents a home may accommodate. By law, care homes are required to display the certificate of registration '*in a conspicuous place*' so that you can see it when you visit.

One of the minimum two inspections carried out each year must be unannounced, but the home must be told when one of the inspections is to take place. Part of the process of inspection is collecting information from people who live there and their relatives about the quality of care. Copies of inspection reports should be available from the CSCI for members of the public to read. If you want to know more about a home, ask for a copy of its latest inspection report.

Private and voluntary care homes

Private care homes are run for profit by private organisations and individual proprietors. Voluntary homes are non-profit-making and run by registered charities, religious organisations and housing associations, sometimes for particular groups of people. Both types of home can choose to whom they offer accommodation.

Local authority care homes

Some care homes are run by the social services department of the local authority. But many authorities have reduced such provision. Local authority care homes have to be registered and inspected by the CSCI and meet the same national minimum standards in exactly the same way as private and voluntary homes.

Care homes (nursing)

Most care homes (nursing) – formerly called nursing homes – are run by private organisations and proprietors, although some are also run by the voluntary sector but not by local authorities. Care homes (nursing) provide nursing care by qualified nurses to people 'suffering from sickness, injury or infirmity'. It is the availability of full-time nursing that makes them different from other care homes. There are a few NHS care homes (nursing), which are sometimes used by the NHS as an alternative to long-stay hospital wards. However, these homes that the NHS provides direct are *not* subject to this system of registration and inspection.

Finding a care home

If the person you are caring for is incapable of making decisions (eg perhaps because of dementia), you will have to decide on their behalf, perhaps with the help of other family members.

If you know of a home that has been recommended by friends, so much the better. However, some people are unsure of how to find a home. Here are some suggestions:

- The CSCI must keep a list of all care homes. You can contact them through the Department of Health (see page 239).
- You can also ask the social services department or a health service Patients Advice and Liaison Services (PALS), which will provide information or tell you how to get it. You could discuss with them any questions you have about going into a home.

Other, local, sources of information include voluntary organisations such as Age Concern and the Citizens Advice Bureau. Some charities and placement agencies help people to find homes. Whilst you may be able to locate a home by other means, some people who wish to find a place quickly, or who live some distance away, find these agencies helpful. The *Yellow Pages* contains addresses and phone numbers of care homes in the area.

Wherever possible, it is advisable to visit a number of homes in order to meet the staff and residents and to find out more about the care that will be provided.

Questions to ask when choosing a home

Problems in finding a home can make it very tempting to accept the first place with a vacancy. If possible, consider and compare more than one home. Try to visit the home, have a good look round, talk to the staff and person in charge and the residents. Some homes will invite you to spend the day at the home, or perhaps to visit to share a meal – ask if this is possible. If you have difficulties travelling to visit homes, contact local voluntary organisations to see if they have volunteer drivers or other transport that could help you.

The home must publish a brochure outlining what it provides, the philosophy of care and the fees it charges. Make sure, however, that the reality of the home matches the brochure and check that you know about all the charges, including those for any additional services. Talk to the residents and see what they are doing. Are they involved in activities and the running of the home? Is there a homely, warm and busy environment? Do the staff seem interested and caring? Make a list of all the personal, practical or nursing tasks that will be needed, together with any important equipment, and ask the home if it will be able to meet these needs. Aim to collect the fullest possible information on a prospective home before making a decision.

Everyone will have different views about what they think is a 'good' home, and each person's needs will differ. Here are some questions you might like to ask. You will have to choose which ones are important for you.

- Are the buildings and grounds well maintained and cared for? Does the home look and smell good?
- Does the home encourage residents to do as much as possible for themselves, and to make choices about as many aspects of their daily lives as they can?
- Do residents have the choice of single or shared rooms? If they share, do they have a say about which resident they share with?
- Are there emergency call systems easily accessible throughout (eg within reach of the bed)?
- Can residents bring personal possessions – furniture, pictures, plants?
- Can the home meet the resident's communication needs – for example, through a language other than English, or non-verbal method such as sign language or large print?
- Do residents choose what and when they will eat? How are special diets catered for? Can residents eat privately with guests from time to time? Have a look at the menus and ask residents what the food is like.
- Can residents prepare any food and drinks for themselves?
- Are residents free to see visitors when and where they choose? Can visitors stay overnight at the home, if they have travelled long distances?
- Can residents use a telephone in privacy, for incoming and outgoing calls?
- Do residents rise and go to bed when they choose? If not, do you consider the arrangements to be reasonable?
- What provision does the home make for taking residents out – on outings, to the shops, to the theatre, to their place of worship, or to entertainment?
- What physical activities are available for residents?
- Is there more than one living room, so that there is a quiet room as well as one with a television?
- Are there books and newspapers available for residents? Do residents visit the library, or does a mobile library come?
- Do the managers of the home ask about how the resident would like to handle their own money or medicines?

- Do residents have their own GPs?
- How will the home let relatives or friends know if a resident is taken ill?
- Is there a residents' committee?
- Does the home encourage residents to say how they feel about living there, and provide written information to residents and/or their families about how to discuss a problem or make a complaint?
- Are toilets available in all parts of the home, fully equipped with handrails and other helpful equipment?
- Can wheelchairs and walking frames go everywhere within the home, and easily in and out?
- Is there a lift? Are there difficult stairs or steps?
- If a resident needs help bathing, does the home have suitable facilities?
- Who will help with bathing or showering, and can the resident choose how often they have a bath or shower?
- Ask about staffing levels – how many staff there are on duty during the day and night, and the ratio of staff to residents over all. Is there a keyworker system where each resident is the special responsibility of a named member of staff?
- Find out whether staff are trained to deal with particular conditions such as Parkinson's disease.
- Watch how staff and residents behave towards each other.
- Are there areas for smoking and non-smoking?
- What happens if residents require more or less care than they currently have? Might they have to leave? What arrangements are made for people who are dying?
- Can residents help in ordinary activities of the home – cleaning, cooking, gardening, looking after pets?

The King's Fund has produced a guide called, *Home from Home*, which advises on how to choose a care home. The Office of Fair Trading has produced a report, *Older People as Consumers in Care Homes*, which is a valuable source of information about good practice, and about areas of bad practice that you might encounter. It also includes useful information on the care home market and the regulatory framework.

Finding a home for a very disabled or mentally frail older person

Some people have difficulty in finding a home for relatives who are very frail – perhaps as a result of a severe stroke – or because of advanced dementia. In some cases a person may be too frail for the average care home but not frail enough for a care home with nursing. In some areas where there are few homes of any sort, it may not be easy to find a place at all. If the local authority assesses the person as needing a place, it should help find an appropriate home. Specialist homes for older people with some kind of mental frailty are often called 'EMI' homes. 'EMI' generally stands for 'Elderly Mentally Infirm', or 'Elderly Mentally Ill'. Such homes specialise in care for older people with a mental illness or disorder – very often, this is for older people who have been diagnosed as having some form of dementia. The brochure published by the care home will describe the kind of care they provide.

Getting care needs assessed

Local authorities have a duty under the NHS and Community Care Act 1990 to carry out an assessment of people who appear to them to need community care services which they may provide or arrange. If you feel you need help that the local authority might be able to arrange – such as home help or home care; respite care; meals at home; or a place in a care home – you can ask the local authority for an assessment. The local authority is obliged to carry out an assessment if it thinks you may need such services. The local authority publishes information about:

- how to ask for an assessment;
- how the assessment will be carried out;
- the kinds of assessment that it may provide;
- the kinds of needs the local authority can help with.

Decisions to make at discharge from hospital

The decision to discharge a patient from hospital is made on the basis of clinical judgement by the consultant (or, in some community hospitals, GPs), taking into consideration the views from the rest of the team caring for that person. The consultant may feel that there is no further treatment in that hospital from which the patient would benefit. However, it is also important that patients are appropriately discharged; if you are worried about the proposal, make an appointment to see the consultant in charge, and clearly describe the reasons why discharge might be inappropriate. Hospitals should have in place proper discharge procedures, and should be able to give you information about this.

If someone is assessed as meeting the criteria for care in a care home, they are expected to pay towards the cost on a means-tested basis. However, the cost of nursing provided by registered nurses in care homes is met by the NHS and will not be included in the fees paid (see below).

Discharge from hospital is now governed by the Community Care (delayed discharge etc) Act 2003. Guidance on implementing the Act (LAC(2003)21:HSC 2003/009) contains specific advice on patient and carer involvement, including:

- consent;
- choice;
- alternative forms of care, such as 'step-down beds', intermediate or recuperative care;
- charging arrangements (which may be discretionary).

Patients do not have a right to stay in an acute hospital bed indefinitely. In these situations, health and social services staff should work with both of you to explore the options, such as care in the person's own home or in sheltered housing, or care in a relative's home. Undue pressure to be moved out of hospital should be resisted if suitable alternative accommodation cannot be found. Nor should anyone feel forced to care for another person if this is not feasible or possible.

If a place in a care home is being arranged by the local authority and there are no vacancies at the home the person wants to move to, they may be discharged to another home or be supported in their own home until a place becomes available.

Paying for care in a care home

Care in a care home is expensive and most people can't afford to pay for it themselves. Most older people living in care homes pay towards the cost of this care; either paying in full themselves from income or capital, or contributing towards the costs according to nationally set means-test rules. The amount the local authority will pay is assessed by social services through a financial assessment, which is separate and different from the assessment of your care needs.

Once the local authority has agreed that the person's care needs require care home provision, the care manager will provide information about the local care homes and encourage the person to make a choice. The local authority makes a contract with the care home. Sometimes, the cost of the chosen care home is higher than the amount the local authority says it pays for the sort of care required. In these circumstances, the person may need to find a 'third party' – such as a relative, friend or charity – to meet the difference, in order to live in that home. However, local authorities cannot set arbitrary ceilings and should be able to show that there are care homes with vacancies at the price they are prepared to pay.

Paying for yourself

Some people have adequate resources to pay for their own care in full. Families may contribute to some or all of the costs, but they do not *have* to do this unless they wish to although a husband or wife might be asked to contribute; see Age Concern Factsheet 39 *Paying for care in a care home if you have a partner*, for more information. If the person has more than a certain amount in capital, they will be expected to pay the full cost of their care in a home.

If you are paying for your own care, or are claiming state benefits, find out whether you might be eligible for Attendance Allowance. Age Concern's Factsheet 10 *Local authority charging procedures for care homes* and Factsheet 34 *Attendance Allowance and Disability Living Allowance* have further information.

127

You can choose which home you move into if you will be making private arrangements, although it will be up to the home whether or not it will offer you a place. Make sure the contract with the home clearly states what the fees include. Make sure, too, that you know how much any 'extras' may cost. Here are some questions you might ask about fees:

■ Is a deposit required? Is this returnable? What is it for?

■ What is the weekly fee, and *exactly* what does this provide?

■ What services are charged for as 'extras'? *Exactly* how much do they cost? ('Extras' can include laundry; hairdressing; chiropody; newspapers; physiotherapy; you will be expected to pay for your own personal items, such as toiletries, clothes, etc.)

■ Would the NHS provide any of these? No one should have to pay for continence products (such as pads) in a care home. They are provided by the NHS. Chiropody and physiotherapy should also be supplied by the NHS if the person has been assessed as needing them.

■ How much notice will the home give if it has to raise the fees?

■ Who is required to sign the contract? (If relatives are asked to sign, they should seek legal advice about what they are committing themselves to.)

■ What fees are payable if the person is away for a short time – say, on holiday or in hospital?

■ How much notice do you need to give the home in order to move? How much notice would you be entitled to if the home closed?

You could also contact the social services department to see if it will tell you how much it pays for a place at the home – care homes often charge private funders more than they charge local authorities. If you find that this is the case, you might be able to negotiate a lower fee.

Finally, although this may be distressing, if you are a relative or friend of someone who is moving to live in a home, you may want to ask the home what payment it expects following a resident's death. Some homes ask for fees to be paid for a short while after the resident's death in order not to have to insist that relatives make the room immediately available by removing all the personal effects on the day of death. However, relatives who have not been aware in advance that an additional payment would be required are often very dis[...] cover this subsequently.

There is one other important issue for self-funders to think ab[...] moving to live in a care home, the person's resources might be redu[...] quite quickly. Although initially they could have enough money to fun[...] themselves, this will drop quite rapidly from paying the home's fees. At that point they will need to ask for help from social services, which might not be willing to fund that place and could require the person to move to a cheaper home. For this reason, it is advisable to get an assessment from the social services department in the first instance. Social services may be able to suggest alternatives to help the person remain at home or in sheltered accommodation; if it is decided that full-time care is needed, social services will advise whether the person will need nursing care or just personal care.

NHS continuing care, free nursing care and intermediate care

When the person you are caring for needs health care, you should consider whether they might be eligible for continuing health care services from the NHS. Eligibility to receive free NHS health care services is based on clinical need, not on ability to pay. In making a decision, a person's health care needs are assessed to see if these needs meet the eligibility criteria set by the 28 Strategic Health Authorities for NHS continuing health care services. NHS continuing health care services are free at the point of use, so the person will not be asked to pay towards these from income or capital. It can be provided in any setting, at home or in a care home. Some people qualify for all of their care home fees to be paid by the NHS if their primary need is for health care.

Nursing care in care homes

Nowadays no one has to pay for care provided by a registered nurse in a care home. The NHS is responsible for paying the nursing home an amount for each individual, based on an assessment by a registered NHS nurse of the care that the resident needs. (In England the amount

...ales there is just one set amount; in Scotland ...the local authority, not the NHS. The NHS is ...ng that any necessary continence pads and ...nt provided by the care home (nursing) are ...harge to the resident.

...ial Care Act 2001 defines nursing care as:

...vided by a registered nurse and involving either the provision of care or the planning, supervision or delegation of the provision of care, other than services which, having regard to their nature and circumstances in which they are provided, do not need to be provided by a registered nurse.'

This means that, although the time spent by a registered nurse in monitoring and supervising work that has been delegated is covered, the time spent by non-registered nurses such as nursing assistants in carrying out that delegated work is not paid for by the NHS.

Continuing NHS health care

'Continuing NHS health care' is the term used when the care a person receives (usually in hospital or a nursing home but it can be in one's own home) is funded in full by the NHS. If someone is in hospital because they have had 'acute' (short-term) treatment – either for a planned operation or as a result of an emergency admission (eg after a fall) – continuing NHS health care is care they receive *after* this acute treatment has finished. As with other NHS health care services, they do not receive continuing NHS health care unless they meet the local eligibility criteria for this service. The NHS can provide continuing NHS health care in a number of ways:

- through a place in an NHS hospital;
- in an NHS care home;
- by the NHS having a contract with a private or voluntary sector care home for the nursing care.

Continuing NHS care also covers free nursing care in all settings, including care homes that provide nursing care; continuing in-patient care in hospital; fully NHS-funded care in care homes; rehabilitation and recovery services including intermediate care, palliative care (see page 132), short-term breaks and specialist transport.

People who are receiving treatment in hospital may need these services before or after they are discharged. But people living in their own homes, in sheltered housing or in care homes may also be able to receive some NHS continuing health care services.

Case study

Peter's wife Pat has dementia and has recently gone into an NHS continuing care bed. Peter said:

'For the first five years I looked after her full-time. I gave up work because I wanted her to have the best.

'The consultants who made the original diagnosis were very helpful. They arranged for her to go to a day centre three days a week, and respite care was always there if I needed a holiday. There was no talk about a care home or me having to pay for it at all. The NHS is paying for all of it and I must say the nurses are wonderful. They said three years ago that there was a continuing care bed for her if I felt I couldn't look after her any more. I always said to myself that I would look after her until I felt that they could do it better ... and that's what happened.

'Well, recently they started talking about her being in the latter stages of the illness so I knew what that meant. When I went to pick her up from a few days in respite I could see she was happy and the staff are just lovely there. It's a long time since she knew who I was and I felt I shouldn't deny her the care she needed. There was no two ways about it really ... they were doing a better job than I could. She's completely bedridden now ... her muscles have wasted so she can't move. They go into a kind of fetal position by the end ... all curled up. She eats well and sleeps well and doesn't show any signs of anxiety at all. She doesn't know any of us and I feel happy that she is really in the best place.

'Knowing that the bed was there all that time if she needed it was a tremendous support to me ... I think it helped me to carry on with that knowledge at the back of my mind. Isolation is the terrible thing when you're a carer. It just goes to show that a supported carer can carry on for much longer.'

Palliative health care

'Palliative health care' is the term used to describe care by a multi-professional team for people (and their families) whose life-threatening disease no longer responds to treatment. Palliative care is concerned with ensuring the best quality of life for the person and their family. This includes controlling pain and other physical symptoms of the disease or illness and, for example, providing emotional support during and beyond the duration of the illness. Palliative care services can be provided by Macmillan nurses employed by NHS Community Trusts; home care nurses, doctors or other health professionals from voluntary or NHS hospices (or from specialist palliative care units); Marie Curie nurses; and a wide range of other voluntary and statutory organisations. Palliative health care can be provided in a variety of settings – for example, in a hospice, in someone's own home, in a care home or in an NHS hospital.

The assessment for NHS nursing care in a care home

The NHS is responsible for meeting the cost of nursing care for people living in care homes that provide nursing care. However, anyone can choose to fund their own nursing care in their care home if they want to.

The amount that the NHS will pay towards an NHS nurse is called the 'Registered Nursing Care Contribution'. A full assessment of care needs will show that:

- care in a home providing nursing is appropriate;
- the person being cared for does not come under the local criteria for NHS fully funded care;
- all other types of care, such as support in the community, have been considered.

The person will then be placed in one of three bands for nursing care, based on a framework of stability, predictability, risk and complexity. Full account must be taken of what is known about the person's condition and their usual behaviour over the course of a week or a number of weeks.

■ **Low band** applies to people whose care needs can be met with minimal input from a registered nurse. Normally it will be paid if the person has chosen to move into a home providing nursing care but their care needs could have been met in another setting with support from a district nurse.

■ **Middle band** applies to people with multiple care needs who require the intervention of a registered nurse on at least a daily basis, and may need access to a nurse at any time. However, their condition should be stable and predictable and likely to remain so.

■ **High band** applies where there are complex needs that require frequent mechanical and/or therapeutic interventions from a registered nurse, and the person's physical or mental health state is unstable or unpredictable.

The amount payable at each of these bands changes every year, so you should seek advice on the amounts.

Challenging the assessment

It has been recognised that in some cases there may be a need for a higher level of nursing care than is covered by the high band, although the person may not meet the local criteria for fully funded continuing NHS health care (ie they can't have their fees paid in full). The Department of Health guidance reminds NHS bodies that they have the responsibility to fund the services the individual needs, and that they should make local arrangements to do so on a case-by-case basis.

If your relative is placed in the highest band (or above), you might wish to question whether they fit the criteria for the NHS to fully fund their care home fees. It will help if you get a copy of the guidance that your local Primary Care Trust has produced. You should be given a copy of a summary of the 'determination of nursing need', which should explain clearly and without the use of jargon, how the nurse has reached the decision. If you are not satisfied with the assessment, you can ask the trust for a review.

133

Currently about 25,300 people in care homes (about 11 per cent) have their fees paid in full by the NHS. Eligibility is based on the nature or complexity or intensity or the unpredictability of an individual's health care needs.

Following the initial assessment, a reassessment will be carried out within three months and annually thereafter. If the person's condition worsens, you can ask for a new determination of nursing need at any time by contacting the nursing home co-ordinator in your area. The nursing home co-ordinator is the person who has been appointed by the local NHS trust to manage NHS-funded nursing care.

If the person goes into hospital, the NHS body will not normally pay for their nursing care in the care home during that period. The contract with the home should explain what the arrangements are for any period such as this. The Government's National Minimum Standards for Care Homes for Older People require that each resident should be provided with a statement of terms and conditions, and self-funding residents with a contract. This should include details of the care and services covered by the fee, the level of fees, extra costs and notice periods. If there is a problem with any aspect of the contract, take the matter up first with the home and then with the local office of the Commission for Social Care Inspection.

If you consider that your relative is not seeing the full advantage of the amount that the NHS is paying for their nursing care, or you do not agree with any arrangements that the home has made, you may wish to complain to the home or the NHS and/or take the matter up with your MP.

Making the transition from home

Moving into a care home is never easy, even if you and the person you care for feel it is the right thing to do. For many people there is a tremendous sense of loss, like a bereavement, about losing their own home. Home is one of the most important places we are attached to. It holds many memories, and our belongings help to give us our identity and self-esteem.

The transition can be made easier if:

- There is time to make short visits beforehand, for a whole day or a short break.
- There are familiar faces – perhaps people that the person already knows.
- The person can take some of their own belongings with them to make their room familiar.
- Any routines such as mealtimes and arrangements for visitors are appropriate.
- The care home is in a familiar neighbourhood.
- The person is able to continue with most former social contacts; eg visiting clubs and societies and keeping in touch with friends.
- You are able to visit easily and take the person out from time to time.
- All your questions have been answered so that everyone is clear about what is going to happen and when.
- You both know how to bring about change if you want to; eg there is a residents' committee where issues are discussed and a complaints procedure that works.

Of course, some of these may not be possible if admission is unexpected and straight from hospital. In such circumstances, your support will be even more important. It will help if you understand some of the feelings involved in such a move and can talk things through with the person after the event.

Many homes have what they call a 'keyworker' scheme. This means that one particular member of staff takes an interest in certain people and takes the lead in making sure that all care needs are being met. This will be the member of staff who draws up or updates the care plan – the document that sets out everything that the person needs and wants from the care home. The keyworker will not always be on duty, of course, so they will not be the only member of staff looking after the person.

It will be important that you continue to be involved in the life of the person you have been caring for even after they have moved into a care home. There may be a support group for the home, a friends and relatives association perhaps. If there isn't one, perhaps you would like to talk to the home about setting one up. The Relatives and Residents Association (contact details on page 252) is a national organisation that offers support and advice to families with a relative in a care home. Some care homes welcome volunteers to be involved in providing activities for the residents, especially during outings. When the home is inspected, you should have the opportunity to contribute your views about the care your relative is receiving.

On the other hand, if you have been caring for someone for a long time, you will be adjusting to a new life yourself. There is nothing wrong with feeling a sense of relief when you are at last able to share the responsibility for care with someone else. You need to get on with your own life, too – pursue new interests and regain your independence.

Nevertheless, someone who is living in a care home needs to have friends and relatives outside keeping an eye on their welfare. Sometimes things can go wrong and your vigilance at those times will be vital. If the person is unhappy with any aspect of their care, your support may be necessary to help get things changed. If it is not possible to sort out the problems by discussing them with the home, maybe the person will want to move to a different care home. This will inevitably be disruptive but sometimes it is the best option.

If a situation arises where you think the welfare of the residents is being put at risk, you should take action. Talk to the care home managers about the problem in the first instance but, if they do not respond in a way that could solve the problem, talk to the Commission for Social Care Inspection (CSCI). The CSCI must investigate complaints about care homes and will act to protect the residents if they believe their welfare is at risk.

Case study

Doris said:

'I'm 94 and I've been a widow for 37 years so I learnt to manage on my own. I had a lovely bungalow with beautiful views which I didn't want to leave. I thought I was coping well. But I was knocked down by a car and broke my leg. After that I couldn't walk very well and my GP suggested a care home. I resisted but I found it difficult to look after myself. It made me so tired just shopping, cooking and keeping the bungalow clean.

'So I went with a friend to visit a number of homes. As soon as we came to this one, we both said, "This is it." I can't put my finger on what it was – it was just the atmosphere … and the garden – that was lovely.

'I put my name down and within a fortnight they had a vacancy. That was a bit sooner than I'd expected and didn't leave me much time to make arrangements. But they were so kind and co-operative. They helped me bring over my own bed and some other furniture. The bed that was in the room went into store and they stored some of my possessions for me, too. As soon as I'd put my pictures up on the walls I felt at home. I went to bed that night and just felt as if I was at home.

'I thought I might be sad when my bungalow was sold because I'd lived there 25 years but I found I didn't mind at all. It was the ending of one part of my life and the start of another. I've no regrets now and no nostalgia. I settled in straight away. They're so kind here. Whatever you ask for – it's no problem. I have a lot of visitors and they always offer a cup of tea. Yes, they're very caring. But do you know what I appreciate most? They give you your freedom.'

Recognising abuse

Abuse is any kind of neglect or exploitation of service users as well as physical violence. Abuse can be:

- Physical – using unnecessary force, rough handling causing bruises, burns or broken bones, restraining someone without their consent, misusing drugs (eg sedatives to control someone).
- Psychological – using threats and creating fear of punishment, making fun of someone, treating adults as though they were children, victimising or insulting someone because of their sexual orientation or racial or ethnic origin.
- Financial – withholding personal property, misusing a service user's money or not allowing someone who could do so to control their own financial affairs.
- Neglect – ignoring care needs; lack of action; leaving someone in a wet bed or not answering their call for help.
- Sexual – forcing someone to take part in any kind of sexual activity against their will or in situations where they are unable to give their consent. Under the Sexual Offences Act 1956, people who have 'an arrested or incomplete development of the mind' are considered to be unable to give consent to sexual activity. This definition may apply to some people with a learning disability.

The principles of good practice should guard against the abuse of service users but, from time to time, perhaps when you least expect it, it happens. Even where there are good relationships and high levels of involvement in decision-making, things can go wrong. Because service users are dependent on their carers, the balance of power is not equal. Abuse usually involves harm by someone who is in a position of power, trust or authority. Staff in a care home are in a position of power over residents.

In the unlikely event that things go wrong, it will be important that you be aware of what's happening and are willing to take action. Contact the CSCI or your local social services department if you are concerned, and they will investigate. Social services departments should have a member of staff who has particular responsibility for investigation into allegations of adult abuse.

Key points

■ The first step is to consider whether it may be possible to stay at home, if this is what you would both prefer, by arranging extra services or care there.

■ If the person you care for lives alone and wants to stay there, you will no doubt be concerned for their welfare. However, remember that many people with care needs live alone very successfully.

■ It is sometimes possible to find a companion, or 'living-in help'. You should consider carefully the duties you require of a companion and write a 'job description' so that there is no misunderstanding by either party about what is expected.

■ Agencies that provide nurses or care workers who carry out personal care tasks have to register with the Commission for Social Care Inspection (CSCI), meet national minimum standards and be inspected every year. Their inspection reports will be published.

■ There are many types of sheltered accommodation available, to rent or to buy, including some with 'extra care'.

■ The decision to go into a care home is not easy. It means that the person you care for has to leave their own home and familiar surroundings. However, there can be real benefits to be gained through new care and companionship.

■ You can do only so much as a carer. If the person you are caring for is unable to look after themselves and/or you are unable to provide the care they need, whatever the reason, a care home is a sensible and realistic option. It is better to arrange proper care for someone than to struggle on until you reach crisis point.

■ All care homes are registered with the CSCI. A distinction is made between care homes and care homes (nursing). Nursing care can be provided only by care homes (nursing). Both kinds of care home provide personal care: washing, bathing, dressing and going to the toilet.

(Continued)

- It can be very tempting to accept the first home with a vacancy. If possible, consider and compare more than one home. Try to visit the home, have a good look round, talk to the staff and person in charge and the residents to find out what it is really like to live there.

- If someone is assessed as meeting the criteria for care in a care home, they are expected to pay towards the cost on a means-tested basis. However, the cost of nursing provided by registered nurses in care homes is met by the NHS and will not be included in the fees paid.

- NHS continuing health care services are free at the point of use – so the person will not be asked to pay towards these from income or capital. They may be provided in hospital or a nursing home or your own home.

- Palliative health care is the term used to describe care by a multi-professional team for people (and their families) whose life-threatening disease no longer responds to treatment. It can be provided in an NHS hospital, a hospice, a care home or your own home.

- Moving into a care home is never easy, even if you and the person you care for feel it is the right thing to do. For many people there is a tremendous sense of loss about leaving their own home. Home is one of the most important places we are attached to. It holds many memories, and our belongings help to give us our identity and self-esteem.

- It is important for you to remain in contact with someone who is living in a care home. Residents need to have friends and relatives outside keeping an eye on their welfare.

- In the unlikely event that things go wrong in a care home, it will be important that you are aware of what's happening and willing to take action.

7 Meeting your own needs

However much you like or love the person you care for, the emotional and physical demands of caring can be extremely stressful. If the person is frail, or has dementia, a chronic or terminal illness, or a serious disability, the demands can be especially great. If you also live with the person, you may feel that you have no time to relax and unwind. Perhaps your feelings of anger, frustration or resentment sometimes get out of control. In this chapter we look at recognising and meeting your own needs as a carer.

Case study

Fred is the main carer for his wife Joan, who has some physical disabilities. He said:

'Joan has difficulty walking and needs to hold on to my arm when we're out. That slows me down of course. I often feel impatient because I am still quite active and I find it difficult to get as much exercise as I'd like. I've noticed that I don't take the dog out for a walk during the day, even though I'd like to. I know Joan would want to come with me but she wouldn't be able to go far and would probably have to wait for me in the car. Then I would feel I couldn't go far, as she's waiting for me. So there's a conflict between what she can do and what I can do. What I tend to do is settle her in front of the television in the evening and then she can accept me going out for an hour and a half or two hours walking with my friend and his dog.

'During the day she just wants me there all the time. I'd like to do more gardening but if she can see me out there she keeps coming to the door and saying: "Isn't it time you came in? Don't overdo it." So I stop long before I really want to. The only way I can go out during the day is to arrange for her to be somewhere else like the Townswomen's Guild or to ask someone to sit with her.'

When faced with an overwhelming set of demands, you may often wish that these pressures would simply go away. If this mountain would get smaller, life would be more manageable. The next step is to turn to the person you care for and wish that they would stop causing you stress. It is only a small step from wishing they would be less demanding to blaming them and feeling resentful about the amount of pressure you think they are putting on you.

Managing the stress of caring

It is only relatively recently that stress has started to be taken seriously in the world of work. Previously the notion of stress was viewed with some suspicion and regarded as something that only a 'wimp' suffered from. Now stress has become a respectable research topic and seen as something that should be taken seriously.

What are your views about stress? Do you view it as something to be ashamed of and keep quiet about or ignore? Are you perhaps viewing it as a fact of life or as something you recognise and want to be able to manage?

Stress is not an inevitable part of life, nor is it something that we just have to put up with. We are much more knowledgeable now about what happens to our bodies when we are stressed. The phrase 'stress-related illness' has entered the general vocabulary. Doctors have

142

become more aware of the effects of stress, which can cause physical illness. Stress also expresses itself through mental and psychological symptoms. At the very least, stress can be an uncomfortable experience and at worst a damaging one for you.

It can also be damaging for the person you care for. If you are feeling stressed, you will not be in the best position to provide the effective care you are capable of giving. The quality of care you provide can diminish and you may pass on your stress to the person you care for.

In this chapter we look at:

■ what stress is;
■ how to recognise the symptoms of stress;
■ what to do about it.

What is stress?

In all areas of our lives we are faced with demands. From the moment we wake up we have to respond to whatever the day (or night) brings. If you are woken suddenly in the night by a noise, your body will probably immediately be on the alert. Perhaps you leap out of bed ready to deal with the emergency. There may be all sorts of things going around in your mind and all sorts of feelings churning around inside you – but is that stress or is it a normal response?

This normal response to emergencies is thought to be part of the basic survival kit of the human body. When our ancestors met danger, they needed to act quickly to survive. The internal alarm button geared them up either to fight or to run away. This is known as the 'fight or flight' response. In many ways this still stands us in good stead. Today we may still find ourselves in situations where there is no time to stand and think over all the available options before making a considered decision. If a car suddenly appears when you are crossing the road, it is sensible to react quickly and get out of the way! Problems only arise when this ancient response is triggered inappropriately.

As human beings we have the ability to respond to the demands made on us. Our brain processes information collected through the senses, which enables us to make decisions. Our emotions enable us to respond to other people and situations. We need a certain amount of stimulation in order to function well and our bodies are designed to deal with it. But everyone responds differently to any particular situation. Stimulation can become stressful when the pressure is too great (or too little) and goes on too long without a break.

Situations where you are bombarded with demands from all directions, over which you have little or no control, are potentially stressful. Because we respond differently, every person needs to find the level of pressure that is appropriate for them (Figure 4). There is a point between boredom and overload that is appropriate for each person. This is the point at which we function best.

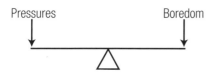

Pressures   Boredom

Figure 4 The balance between too much pressure and boredom

The aim of stress management is to keep the pressures at an optimum level so that we are always functioning at our best. The important factors are:

■ the level of pressure – whether real or perceived, from outside or inside (eg self-imposed);

■ your level of resilience – affected by past experience, self-confidence, skill levels, quality of support;

■ how long the pressure lasts – left unmanaged for a long period of time, pressures can become damaging.

Recognising the signs

A great deal of research has been carried out to try to find ways to measure stress. Researchers have tried:

- taking physiological measurements of muscle tension;
- measuring biochemicals in the bloodstream;
- self-reports using questionnaires.

The results have been variable. The important thing we want to emphasise here is for you to recognise the signs that tell you when you are stressed so that you can do something about it. Get to know your own body.

The 'fight or flight' response to pressure, which we mentioned earlier, produces lots of visible physical changes in the body (Figure 5). To run away or fight, the blood needs to be pumped round faster to the muscles of the arms and legs. So the heart rate increases and breathing becomes more shallow and rapid to ensure a good intake of oxygen. The muscles of the shoulders and neck tighten and the body weight swings forward onto the balls of the feet. One of the side-effects of this is that the digestive system slows down, as food becomes less of a priority. There may be a 'butterfly' sensation in the stomach and sweating begins as a way of cooling the body down. The hormones released during this process raise anxiety and a range of other feelings that can make us irritable or short-tempered. We have learnt to fight with words and facial expression or gesture rather than fists. On the other hand, we may become withdrawn and feel less like communicating even if we don't run away.

Do you recognise any of these symptoms? Make a note of any that you particularly notice in your own body.

We are designed to face danger from time to time. However, we are not designed to constantly face today's equivalent of the woolly mammoth all day, every day. The dangers if stress is left unmanaged can be real physical illnesses, for example:

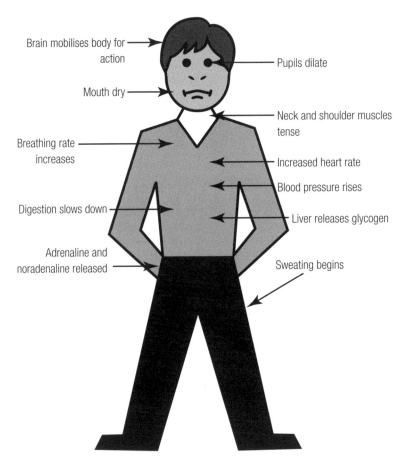

Figure 5 How the body prepares for 'fight or flight'

■ heart problems can result from constant over-stimulation;

■ the digestive system can run into problems if the blood supply is constantly diverted to somewhere elsewhere in the body;

■ the immune system slows down, making us more prone to infection.

So, if you recognise that you are becoming inappropriately stressed, it is important to do something about it.

Changes brought about by stress

We have described what happens to the body in response to danger. The important thing for you to learn is how stress affects you – how to recognise what is happening. When the pressures build up and move away from the optimum level, which is different for each person, changes start to occur.

These changes can be experienced or show themselves in many different areas of functioning:

■ changes in mental functioning;
■ changes in behaviour;
■ changes in emotions;
■ physical changes.

Case studies

> **Laura** noticed that sometimes she got a 'fuzzy' feeling in her brain and noticed that her memory was not functioning normally. She had to keep writing things down to make sure she didn't forget them ... and then forgot to look at the list.
>
> **Paul** described stress purely in terms of the feelings he became aware of. When stress was around for him he began to feel anxious, less confident and angry at the smallest things.

If you are in contact with other people, comments from them can draw your attention to changes in behaviour. But if you are relatively isolated, as carers often are, you may not get that feedback except from the person you are caring for.

Changes in mental functioning can take the form of:

■ difficulty in absorbing information;
■ difficulty in concentrating;

147

- attention wandering;
- difficulty in making decisions;
- impaired judgement – making 'bad' decisions.

Changes in behaviour include:

- difficulty in managing time – always being late for appointments;
- relying on alcohol or drugs;
- having difficulty sleeping;
- more aggressive behaviour;
- less communicative.

Changes in emotions can include:

- feeling anxious;
- loss of self-confidence;
- feeling panicky;
- feeling irritable and short-tempered;
- reduced libido.

Physical changes can take the form of:

- strained back;
- headaches and migraine;
- indigestion and digestive problems;
- susceptibility to colds and other infections;
- increased heart rate – palpitations.

The aim is to recognise at an early point when pressure levels are moving away from the optimum for you. Once you have started to identify the symptoms that can tell you that stress is becoming a problem, you will be able to use that information again in the future. Try to listen to those around you without getting defensive. Sometimes the changes can develop quite gradually, so it is important to listen to your body and pick up on the clues as early as possible.

Feelings

Everyone reacts differently to the stresses of caring. But when carers get together, they often find that they share many of the same feelings. It can be very reassuring to talk to other carers and discover that your feelings are quite 'normal' for your situation. Some of the common feelings carers describe are:

- frustration
- resentment
- guilt
- anger
- fear
- loneliness
- depression.

Let's look at ways of dealing with feelings like these.

Frustration

Any carer knows how frustrating it can be to look after someone who is ill or disabled. The demands of the daily routine of caring can leave you feeling constantly thwarted. For example, you might not be able to go out when you want to. You may not be able to invite people to visit you. The person you are caring for may not always seem very grateful or acknowledge all the help you give them. If their health is gradually deteriorating, you may find their increasing dependence on you frustrating and exasperating.

The person you are caring for may be feeling frustrated, too, of course. They might have led a full and independent life before illness or disability struck. Between you, you need to find ways in which you can lead more separate lives. The person you are caring for may need to be allowed more independence or freedom, perhaps through extra outside help or additional aids or adaptations.

149

Resentment

Resentment can be linked closely with frustration. It's easy to feel resentful if all your time and energy seem to be taken up by someone else, especially if they do not seem to appreciate your help. People who are ill or in pain are not always easy to live with, and this might make you feel even more resentful. Often you will have to cope with the conflicting emotions of love and resentment at the same time. It is important not to let your resentment build up.

Guilt

Most of us have feelings of guilt at times. We might think that we have let someone down or not done as much as we could have. Feelings of guilt can be especially strong in carers who often feel that, however much they do, it is not enough. This can be particularly difficult for people who look after one or both of their parents. You may feel that you owe something to your parents that you can never pay back properly.

Try not to let feelings of guilt get out of proportion. Remind yourself about what you have done that was good and positive for the person you are caring for. For example, you might have washed an elderly relative's hair once a week for the past five years. You might wish you had done more for her but that one small weekly commitment could have made all the difference to her quality of life. The best advice is to admit to your feelings of guilt and try to get them out into the open. A close friend or family member may be able to reassure you, or perhaps someone outside the situation could help you get your feelings back into perspective.

Anger

You may be feeling very angry about your situation as a carer. You may have had to take on the role of caring unwillingly or at a difficult time of your life. Perhaps you had small children to look after as well, maybe your career was just about to take off or you were looking forward to a restful retirement.

150

Some carers find their feelings of anger about the situation begin to be directed towards the person they are caring for rather than at the situation itself. This can lead to conflict and tension. Some difficult days are to be expected, especially if you are together most of the time and perhaps you are not getting enough sleep. But you do need to find a way of coping with your feelings of anger before they become impossible to control.

If you can, talk with the person you are caring for about how you feel when you are angry and the things that make you feel especially angry. They might be feeling angry with you, too. Together you might be able to work out ways to avoid clashes. If you can't talk to each other, try to find someone outside the situation to talk to.

Fear

Illness or disability can be frightening, especially if you feel you have no control over what's happening. You might be afraid of the future, perhaps you don't know how the person's illness or disability will progress or you are worried that you will be left alone when the person you are caring for dies. Feelings of fear can keep you awake at night, when they often seem to magnify and become insurmountable in your mind.

Remember that you can phone the Samaritans (details on page 254) during the night as well as during the day. Try to get your fears out into the open in the daytime by talking about them with someone you can trust. Often just talking is enough to make you feel better.

Loneliness

It is easy to become isolated if you are caring for someone, especially someone who needs a lot of attention. Socialising might be right at the bottom of your list of priorities when there are so many other demands on your time. It might seem easier to stay at home and avoid making arrangements to see anyone else. But in the long term you may regret it.

Loneliness is one of the biggest problems for carers. However difficult it may seem, try to make sure you see other people at least once or twice a week. It could be someone in your family, a friend or perhaps someone

151

from a local self-help or carers' group. You might be surprised by the difference that regular contact with people outside your situation can make to your life.

Depression

Most carers have bad days when they feel sad, lonely or anxious. This is especially likely if the person you are caring for demands a lot of attention or you are having interrupted nights. Most people find that the bad times don't last forever and they are able to pick themselves up again after a few days. But if you find that you often feel desperate or anxious and can't get back on an even keel, you need to get some help. There is nothing to be ashamed of – you are only feeling as you do because of your situation. It is important not to struggle on to the point where you are unable to continue caring because you are too depressed. Find someone you can talk to about how you feel. If you can't talk to your family or friends, get some professional help, perhaps from your GP or a counsellor.

Pressures we put on ourselves

There are some common pressures associated with the role of carer that we can put on ourselves:

- putting others first and ignoring our own needs;
- the perfectionist streak;
- never asking for help;
- doing everything quickly, whether speed is required or not;
- turning everything into a struggle.

Putting others first

Being concerned about the needs of other people is an integral part of being a carer. It would be very difficult to take on the role if you had no thought or consideration for others. However, this is not the same as taking the view that it is only the needs of the other person that matter.

The message that many women in particular learn as they grow up is that other people's needs should come first. They may grow up expecting to be the carer in the family and not believe that their own aspirations and needs have any value. It is not easy to get the balance right between your needs and those of the person you care for but it *is* possible and vital to take account of both.

The perfectionist streak

Most people take pride in doing a good job – it makes them feel they are of value. But it can be taken to extremes when it becomes a demand for perfection. Of course, mistakes in the context of caring can be costly in human terms and should be avoided wherever possible but no one is perfect. Striving to do a good job is a necessary pressure but striving for perfection is unnecessary and unachievable.

Never asking for help

A lot of people have a strong wish to stand on their own feet and be independent. Independence is often regarded as desirable and generally a good thing. But sometimes it can be taken too far. If you can't allow yourself to ask for help, that is potentially a problem. Asking for help and support when appropriate is a useful skill in managing pressure. It can become difficult to do if the demand inside you is for total independence.

Doing everything quickly

Sometimes our relationship with time becomes distorted. We may feel we have to beat the clock, trying always to get more and more done at a faster pace. Getting ahead of ourselves can mean preparing for the next task in the schedule instead of taking a well-earned rest. There might be an advantage in peeling the vegetables for lunch while still eating breakfast, if you then put your feet up to enjoy that last cup of tea. Life can too easily be led at a hurried pace. There are tasks that need to be done quickly and where speed is essential but there are also tasks that improve from taking more time. The skill is in understanding the difference between the two and behaving appropriately. There are no prizes for completing everything in record time and it is one sure way of creating stress.

Everything must be a struggle

In this version of demand from within, the key message is that every task must require a lot of effort. It is like the old school reports that said: 'Must try harder' because the effort was seen as important whether or not the task required it. As with doing everything at speed, the skill is in distinguishing between tasks that require a lot of effort and those that don't. Some tasks benefit from taking a more relaxed approach.

Practising key skills to reduce pressure

Three key skills in reducing unnecessary pressure are:

■ being able to refuse requests and say 'no' assertively;
■ expressing your wants and needs clearly and assertively;
■ setting clear boundaries around your role as a carer.

Part of each of us is the 'internal dialogue' that accompanies us in everything we do. It is the conversation we have running in our heads. We do not need another person present for us to be involved in a lengthy debate about everything that happens to us. It has been said that talking to yourself is a sign of madness. But the internal dialogue does not usually take place out loud and it is perfectly normal. It has been described as being like having the radio on low all the time.

The internal dialogue plays an important part in creating stress by affecting our response to pressure. It can lead us to worry unnecessarily by expecting that events will turn out badly. The internal dialogue plays a part in:

■ how we perceive what is happening now;
■ how we look ahead to the future;
■ the sense we make of the past.

Each of us has a set of unwritten rules about how the world is and how we should behave in it. These 'rules' or beliefs are learnt during child-hood and quite difficult to change. Often we don't know what is stored in our internal dialogue. We may have been acting in a particular way for years and lost track of the fact that our behaviour is based on our own personal set of unwritten rules. There are three steps to take:

- identify the unwritten rules in your internal dialogue;
- learn to question your unwritten rules;
- learn to substitute more helpful permisions to yourself.

Learning to say 'no'

For many people, saying 'no' is just not part of their repertoire. If you have difficulty saying 'no' to impossible requests, you may have an internal dialogue that is telling you: 'If someone asks you to do some-thing, you must always do it.'

If you agree to every request, it won't be long before you are over-loaded. You have to convince yourself somehow that saying 'no' is okay and a reasonable response if you are already overloaded. The abil-ity to say 'no' is a useful skill to learn:

- try to become aware of your internal dialogue;
- question your internal dialogue – ask yourself if this belief you have stored away still holds good today;
- substitute something that is more likely to encourage you to protect yourself;
- practise using the words.

> Find a quiet place and take a few moments on your own. Think of a situation where you wanted to say 'no' but didn't. What was happening in your head? How could you have put things differently? What are the words you should have used? Write them down and practise saying them out loud in front of the mirror. If you can find a friend to practise with, that would help even more.

There are two principles that underpin putting these skills into practice:

- Be aware of both your verbal and non-verbal behaviour – we communicate not only through the words we use but through gestures, facial expressions or the way we dress as well. Both forms of communication need attention if we are to give a clear message.
- Use words and actions that treat the other person positively, with dignity and as an equal.

To say 'no', you have to know what you want and need. The first step is to give yourself permission to have your own wants and needs. The next step is to express them clearly. There are lots of possible beliefs that can stop you expressing your wants and needs:

- This person is hard of hearing and won't hear what I say.
- This person never listens to a word I say, so there's no point in speaking.
- It is kinder not to say anything. I will just make it look as though I am agreeing and then not do it – she won't remember.

The more specific you can be in identifying what is holding you back, the more chance you have of removing the barrier.

Setting boundaries around your caring role is not easy for family carers. You need to have a clear picture of who you are and your wants and needs, which can be difficult when you are caring for a relative, especially a parent.

Providing care for someone does not mean you are available 24 hours a day 7 days a week, although it may often feel as though there is no getting away from your caring responsibilities. Your time needs careful management if you are to get some respite. Saying 'no' is much harder if the boundaries are not clear.

Quick responses to dealing with stress

There are many techniques to defuse stress as it happens. Some of them are suitable to use on the spot as soon as you realise your stress response has swung into action. No one around you will know what you are doing but you will feel the difference. The stress response starts in the mind, so that is where you can begin to tackle it by changing the picture you have of the issue.

- Making the stressful object or factor silly – if the 'dangerous beast' is a person, pause, blink and then try to imagine them as an animal. The image of a docile tabby cat may take the edge off the tension. Think of an image you like and store it up for future use.
- Retreating to a calm, peaceful place – create an image of a particularly calm, pleasurable place, such as a beach, countryside scene or a favourite haunt. When you have thought of a couple of examples, store them away for future use. In a crisis, pause, blink and allow the image of your favourite place to enter your mind. This will take your mind away from what is actually happening and help restore a sense of proportion to your reaction.

Releasing the pressure, relaxation and exercise

Our reactions to stress are rooted in the perfectly normal response to physical attack – for example, to prepare us for 'fight or flight'. A long period of stress can result in exhaustion, migraines, aches and pains, digestive problems and a low resistance to infections. Constantly having these symptoms is in itself stressful and so the cycle continues. Eventually, even the most minor setback is likely to cause extreme anger or a flood of tears. When this happens, your body is giving you a warning. Carers often say they can't slow down because of the person they care for. But you must learn to listen to your body. If it is telling you there is something wrong with your lifestyle, the result of not listening can be major illness.

A very important way of dealing with stress is to learn how to relax. You can do this by:

- releasing the pressure;
- relaxation techniques;
- exercise.

Releasing the pressure

You could liken these techniques to the valve on a pressure cooker, which lets out a sudden burst of steam when the pressure reaches a certain level. Knowing how to release the pressure can give you confidence in your ability to deal with stress. There are three methods we can suggest:

- Hitting a safe object – the wish to do battle is a common response to stress. It is one reason why slamming doors is a common component of rows. Find a safe place to vent your anger safely – for example, by hitting a pillow or cushion in short sharp swings, letting the tension go down your arm and out of your fist. Forcing the air out of your lungs in a shout as you do it strengthens the impact of releasing the pressure. Throwing stones in the sea can be equally satisfying, but not much help if you live inland.
- Shouting inside your head – this can be used when there are other people around. Tune in to the voice in your head and turn up the volume silently. Some people find it helpful to silently shout 'no' or 'stop' in their heads as a way of feeling more in control of difficult situations.
- Writing it out – on paper or on a computer screen, write down everything you would like to say, all you want to get off your chest. This shifts the pressure out of your body and onto the page. Don't send it to anyone. Tear it up or keep it in a safe place. The simple activity of writing things down and transferring your inner feelings in a daily or weekly diary can be a good way to release tension.

Relaxation techniques

One of the good things about your body is that you can encourage it to become more relaxed. When stress strikes, our breathing rate increases and becomes more shallow. Breathing exercises concentrate on slowing down the breathing and making it deeper:

1   Sit or lie comfortably on the floor, in bed or in the bath.
2   Breathe in, count one, then breathe out counting one.
3   Breathe in, count one, two, then breathe out counting one, two.
4   Keep going slowly and regularly until you get to at least five.

The aim is to empty your mind of everything but your deep and regular breathing. Saying the numbers means that your brain can't focus on anything else. If you find unwanted thoughts creeping in, start breathing again at 'one' and try again. With enough practice it will eventually become second nature and you will be able to relax whenever you need. In a crisis, taking one good long deep breath and then forcing the air out strongly can calm us down immediately.

Another technique that can be used without anyone else being aware of what you are doing is to bring the tension level in your muscles under conscious control. As the stress response gets going, the tension in the muscles increases. To reverse the process, first become aware of the build-up of tension in your muscles. You may feel it in your neck or per-haps you grit your teeth or clench your fists. Wherever you feel it, exaggerate the tension and then let go. Letting go needs to be a strong positive movement. Your body will respond to the letting go of muscle tension.

Day and evening classes in relaxation techniques such as yoga are avail-able in most areas. Your local library or adult education centre should have details. Perhaps you can arrange a 'sitter' so that you can attend.

Complementary therapies

The terms 'complementary therapy' or 'alternative medicine' are used to describe a range of treatments available from practitioners and ther-apists; they may work alongside doctors in conventional medicine but often practise outside the NHS. Most of them use methods that aim to treat the whole body and are intended to complement orthodox medi-cine. One of the areas where they can be particularly successful is stress relief.

Case study

Janet said:

'My daughter encouraged me to have a weekly treat while my husband was at his physiotherapy session, so I went to an aromatherapist – it was wonderful. The therapist made me feel special and I came out feeling like I was floating on air. It was better than a holiday – that time for myself made all the difference.'

Useful therapies for stress relief include:

- Aromatherapy – uses essential oils to induce a sense of well-being and relaxation.
- Massage – invigorates and tones the body, releasing tension in areas such as the neck and shoulders.
- Reflexology – uses the power of touch to apply gentle pressure to different parts of the soles of the feet that are said to relate to parts of the body.
- Meditation – develops the capacity of the brain to concentrate through complete relaxation in mind and body.
- Hypnotherapy – induces a trance-like state to bring about physical and mental changes.

It is important to make sure you go to someone who is experienced and qualified to practise in their field. Local GP surgeries and health centres sometimes have lists of reputable therapists. You may sometimes be able to get complementary therapies paid for by the NHS through a GP referral but often you will have to pay for the service. Alternatively, you can go to the national bodies responsible for providing training and recognition. Practitioners may advertise in the telephone directory or on the internet – look for qualifications and membership of recognised bodies. Getting a recommendation from a friend or someone whose judgement you trust is a good guide.

Exercise

It is not helpful to stand stock still when the stress response is raging. Even if you only walk from room to room, movement will help calm your body.

Vigorous physical exercise can also help you relax. The physical effort helps to unwind tight muscles, with the result that your body feels more relaxed afterwards and you have a general feeling of well-being. A longer bout of exercise at the end of the day can be a very effective way of keeping you on an even keel. It need not take long – 15 or 20 minutes is enough to calm the body down. It has been said that the best form of exercise machine is a dog! Being fitter can also help you with the physical demands of caring. Any kind of vigorous exercise will help – walking briskly, swimming, cycling or a keep-fit class. It is important to choose a form of exercise that suits you. Don't add to the stress by trying to force yourself to do something you don't enjoy. Again, your local library or local newspaper should have details of what is available locally.

Increasing your resilience

We all react to stress in our own individual way, and one of the factors in this response is our level of resilience. This level depends on many factors:

- past experience;
- self-confidence;
- skill levels;
- quality of support.

Resilience is not fixed: it varies from time to time. If your resilience is high at a particular time, you will be able to cope with a greater level of pressure. If your resilience is low for some reason, you will experience stress symptoms sooner. Working on your resilience takes time, effort and a belief that it is a worthwhile thing to do.

Whatever strategy you adopt to boost your resilience, the one essential that has to be in place is a belief in the importance of taking care of yourself. This is not always easy to do when you spend your time taking care of others. Try the following activity to find out what your beliefs are about caring for yourself.

How easy do you find it to take care of yourself?

Read through the following statements and tick whether you agree or disagree with each one. Even if it is hard, try to give an answer one way or the other.

	Statement	(a) agree	(b) disagree
1	It is always better to spend my time on others rather than on myself		
2	Looking after myself is sensible		
3	What I want or need for myself is less important than what others want from me		
4	I am important and my needs are important		
5	Looking after myself is selfish		
6	I deserve attention from myself		
7	I am not worth spending time on and looking after		
8	I must look after myself because only then am I in a fit state to look after other people		
9	No grown person should need looking after; only children need looking after		
10	Other people matter but so do I		
11	Other people matter more than I do		
12	Everybody needs looking after, whatever their age		(Continued)

13 If I do require some care and attention, I will have to fight for it		
14 If I need some care and attention, it is up to me to be assertive in asking for what I need		

Scoring

Give yourself 3 points for each of the following answers:

1b, 2a, 3b, 4a, 5b, 6a, 7b, 8a, 9b, 10a, 11b, 12a, 13b, 14a.

The maximum score is 42.

If you scored between 30 and 42 you have a set of beliefs and values that will help you to take care of yourself.

If you scored between 21 and 30 you have some views that could get in the way of your care for yourself. You may need to re-evaluate these before you can plan an effective strategy.

If you scored less than 21 it is likely you will find it hard to plan a programme for looking after yourself. The values and beliefs you hold will get in the way of devising a constructive strategy. So, for the sake of the person you care for, you need to do some work on your attitude towards the way you value yourself.

The notion of balance underpins most of what we have said about managing stress. It is important to get balance in your life between negative pressures and positive pleasures. Ensuring that you have stability zones in your life will help a great deal. These are not just constants, like religious beliefs or supportive people and organisations that are always there when you need them. They are also places where you get good feelings, recognition and the joy of being yourself. Caring can be rewarding as well as demanding so, if you are lucky, some of these good feelings will come through caring as well as through 'play'. Having good stability zones in your life will counter the negative experiences of some of the demands you face. Stability zones can be linked to:

- people
- places
- things

- ideas
- activities
- organisations

What stability zones do you have in your life?

Find a paper and pencil and a quiet place to work. Try to answer the following questions.

1   What values and beliefs do you hold that provide you with a secure base?

2   What places, large or small, provide you with roots or security?

3   Who are the people in your life on whom you rely and who act as stability zones for you?

4   What are the things with which you feel comfortable and which act as stability zones?

5   What activities do you do that act as stability zones and anchors in your life?

6   What organisations or groups provide you with a sense of belonging?

Look back over your answers and see whether you can answer questions A, B and C below:

A   Do you need to change the patterns of your stability zones?

B   Are there any changes that you would like to make in the pattern of your stability zones? Do you have enough of them? Are they reliable and will they serve you in the future?

C   If you have identified any changes you would like to make, how are you going to make them happen?

The key words for resilience are: support, competence, confidence and balance.

Talking it over

One of the best ways of dealing with stress is to talk about it. However, many people find this difficult, perhaps because they:

■ think they are letting themselves down if they admit that they are under stress;
■ feel they would be betraying the person they are caring for if they talk about their problems to anyone else;
■ are worried about breaking down and crying in front of someone else;
■ are not used to discussing their feelings with other people;
■ can't see the point.

If you don't talk about how you feel, your feelings can easily get out of proportion. It's surprising how much it can help just to have shared how you feel with someone.

Networks of support are vital to everyone: family, friends, organisations, neighbours and professionals.

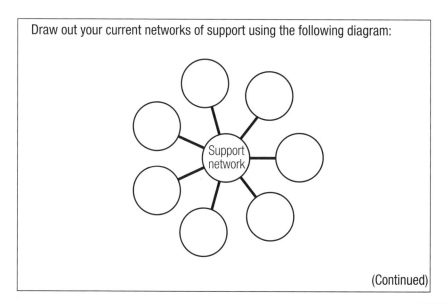

Draw out your current networks of support using the following diagram:

Support network

(Continued)

Now answer the following questions:

■ Which are the areas you feel you need to develop further?

■ Are there family members or friends that you have not been in touch with for a long time?

■ Have you looked around in your locality for organisations that could help?

■ Could your relationships with professionals be developed further?

■ Are you asking for all the help you need?

Whom you talk to will depend on your situation. Try to choose someone you know you can trust and who will listen sympathetically. This is not the time to be told to 'pull your socks up'. You need encouragement and support. For example, you might decide to talk to:

■ A member of your family – they might understand your situation best.
■ A close friend – they may know you well enough to give honest advice.
■ Another carer – they may well have experienced something similar themselves.
■ A GP or social worker – they may be very familiar with your situation and the needs of the person you are caring for.
■ The Samaritans – they are independent of the situation and always there. You can talk to a trained volunteer in confidence about anything (contact details on page 254).

If you don't know any other carers, think about joining a local carers' group or a self-help group. You can find out more from Carers UK (contact details on page 262).

Getting counselling

If you find it difficult to talk about your feelings with someone you know, you might like to try counselling. Talking to a trained counsellor may help you explore aspects of your situation more openly and honestly than you can with people you know. A counsellor will not be involved in your situation and will be able to guarantee that whatever you say will be private and confidential. A counsellor will not judge you or tell you what to do but will help you look at your life and your relationships in a way that you might not have done before, so that you can see things more clearly and respond differently to your situation. Having counselling is not a sign of failure. It's a first positive step towards getting help and feeling better about yourself and your life.

If you think counselling can help, you can:

- Ask your GP. They sometimes provide counselling themselves or can refer you on to someone else on the NHS.
- Contact a voluntary organisation such as Relate (details on page 252). There are many organisations that provide counselling for different situations; sometimes it is free but there is often a sliding scale of charges depending on your ability to pay. Ask your Citizens Advice Bureau for information about local groups or ring Carers UK's CarersLine for information about national organisations that might have branches in your area.
- Pay a private counsellor. There are private counsellors all over the UK, some working within groups and others independently. There are lots of different kinds of counselling and you need to be sure that the counsellor you choose is qualified in their field. You can get a list of private counsellors in your area from the British Association for Counselling and Psychotherapy (contact details on page 231).
- Ring the Samaritans. They are available any time, free of charge.

Making changes in your life

If you have tried everything and you still feel under stress, it might be time to look again at your situation. Think very carefully about whether you can go on caring. If the honest answer is 'no', try not to feel that you have failed in some way. It is better to be realistic and make good alternative arrangements than carry on regardless until you collapse.

There may be other options that will allow you to reduce the burden of caring without giving up altogether; for example, getting additional help at home or regular respite. There could be a day centre nearby or a sitting service that could share the care with you. Make sure you have time for yourself. Letting go of some of the practical problems of caring might give you more 'quality time' with the person you care for. Alternatively, it may be time to start thinking about the possibility of a care home. A local authority assessment might help to clarify the options open to you and the person you care for. (See Chapter 6 for more details on longer term options.)

Making changes in your life may seem daunting. Changes of any kind bring their own pressures – to adapt and find new ways of doing things. You do not have to change your role, give up caring or move house in order to begin to plan for a life that provides optimum pressure without stress.

Five steps to change

Bringing about changes in your own patterns of life involves five steps:

Step 5:	Increase the practice until it becomes part of your normal repertoire.
Step 4:	Get feedback from others on how you are doing.
Step 3:	Practise in small ways to start with.
Step 2:	Identify the behaviour you want to learn.
Step 1:	Recognise your existing patterns.

It might sound simple but it will not be easy. Recognising your existing patterns of behaviour can be quite a searching activity. After all, they will be patterns that have built up over many years. Recognising the unhelpful messages that we give ourselves can sometimes be quite painful. It is always useful to enlist some support for this process, just as you might join a slimming club if you wanted to lose weight.

You do not have to continue to suffer. A key point to emphasise is that, whatever your experience of pressure and stress has been, it is possible to develop new ways of dealing with it and managing yourself. Above all, having a sense of being more in control of your pressures should in itself increase your resilience. Being aware that there are things you can do and strategies and techniques available will help you feel more optimistic and more able to care.

Key points

■ However much you like or love the person you care for, the emotional and physical demands of caring can be extremely stressful.

■ It is only a small step from wishing the person you care for would be less demanding to blaming them and feeling resentful about the amount of pressure you think they are putting on you.

■ Stress has become a respectable research topic and seen as something that should be taken seriously.

■ Stress is not an inevitable part of life, nor is it something that we just have to put up with. It can cause damaging physical and emotional symptoms, and should be tackled before it injures your health and makes you a less effective carer.

■ Everyone reacts differently to the stresses of caring. But when carers get together they often find that they share many of the same feelings of frustration, resentment, guilt, anger, fear, loneliness or depression.

■ Sometimes we put pressures associated with the role of carer onto ourselves.

■ A very important way of dealing with stress is to learn how to relax. You can do this through releasing the pressure, relaxation techniques and exercise.

■ It is important to get balance in your life between negative pressures and positive pleasures.

■ Become aware of your stability zones.

■ Networks of support are vital to everyone: family, friends, organisations, neighbours and professionals.

■ If you find it difficult to talk about your feelings with someone you know, you might like to try talking to a trained counsellor.

8 What to do if someone dies

You may have been a carer for many years or only for a short time. The person you are caring for may have had a long life or still be relatively young. Whatever the situation, your own needs and concerns will be personal to you and different from anyone else's. In this chapter we highlight some of the issues that arise for most carers when the person they are caring for dies. We look first at some of the practical things that you will need to do. Then we look at some of the feelings that are very common when someone dies and what you can do to come to terms with the changes in your life.

Immediate practical things to do

If the person you are caring for dies in hospital or a hospice, there will be people around to advise you on what to do. If it happens at home, you may not find that kind of support so this is the area we focus on here. There are lots of arrangements and practical things to see to. The Department for Work and Pensions publishes a free booklet: *What to do after a death: a guide to what you must do and help you can get*. This details all the practical and legal matters you will have to deal with.

Call the doctor (not an ambulance)

If someone dies at home, the GP who has been looking after them can confirm the death and issue two things:

- a Medical Certificate of cause of death;
- a Formal Notice explaining how to register a death.

If the GP has not seen the person within the previous 14 days or is uncertain about the cause of death, the coroner (procurator fiscal in Scotland) must be notified and a post-mortem examination will be done to find the cause of death. There is no need to be anxious about a post-mortem and it should not delay the funeral arrangements. If there is to be a cremation, the funeral director or GP will need to arrange for a second form to be signed by another doctor.

Organ donation

Some people carry organ donor cards making their wishes clear, and many others would be willing to allow their organs to be used but haven't got around to getting a card. If this is an issue you discussed with the person you cared for, you will be able to carry out their wishes. You need to contact the nearest hospital as soon as possible so that the organs can be removed quickly. If the death happens in hospital, the doctor or ward sister should be told so that they can help to make the necessary arrangements.

Registering the death

Deaths have to be registered within five days in the area in which the death occurred (eight days in Scotland). You do not have to attend the Register Office in the district where the death occurred; you can make a formal declaration, giving all the details required, in any registration district. This information will then be passed to the Registrar for the district where the death occurred, who will issue the death certificate and other documents. If there is a post-mortem or inquest, the time limit is different but the coroner will explain that.

When you get the Medical Certificate you should also be given information about where the local Register Office is and the times of opening. If not, you can find it in the phone book under 'Registration of Births, Deaths and Marriages'. The Registrar may require you to make an appointment to register the death. You don't have to register the death yourself – another relative can do it for you. The person who registers the death will need to take:

■ the Medical Certificate showing cause of death;
■ birth certificate (if available);
■ marriage certificate (if relevant);
■ medical card (if available);
■ pension book (if any);
■ benefits books (if any).

This information is used by the Registrar to complete the formalities. Once the death has been registered, a white certificate is issued free of charge; it contains a social security form to claim any arrears of benefits due to the estate of the deceased person and to ensure that the correct benefits are paid to the widow (if applicable). You will also receive a Certificate for Burial or Cremation: this must be given to the funeral director.

It is a good idea to ask for extra copies of the death certificate at the time of registering the death, as you will need several copies for dealing with the Will and other business such as banks and building societies. You will have to pay for these copies.

Arranging a funeral

You do not have to hold a funeral immediately unless you want to. It may be helpful to wait for a while to make sure that the arrangements are exactly what your relative (or you) wanted and to give some notice to the people who want to be there. However, you should contact the funeral director straight away. They can be very helpful both in arranging the funeral and in advising you on all the official forms and processes.

173

They will collect the person who has died from the hospital or your home and keep him or her until the funeral.

Even simple funerals can cost quite a lot. You should get quotes from at least two funeral directors, making sure that everything is included (church or crematorium fees, cars, flowers, organist, etc). Find out how you are going to pay for the funeral before you go ahead with the arrangements. The costs can be paid out of the estate of the person who has died (the 'estate' includes their money, property and possessions). However, it may be some time before that money is available and the funeral director will probably need payment before then.

Often the bank or building society will be prepared to pay funeral costs from the account of the person who has died even before probate has been granted (see below). They make out a cheque direct to the funeral director's firm. There are other possible sources of funds:

- Some people take out a prepayment funeral plan.
- Some personal pension schemes and insurance plans include a lump sum for funeral costs.
- National Savings accounts may release money for funeral costs.
- Some trades unions or professional associations pay a benefit when a member dies.
- If you are receiving some forms of state benefit, you may get help from the Social Fund. You can claim this up to three months after the funeral.

The Department for Work and Pensions, Citizens Advice Bureau or Carers UK's CarersLine should be able to help you find out whether you are eligible for help from the Social Fund. However, if other members of your family could pay for the funeral, even if they don't want to, your application may be turned down.

If you are not eligible for financial help from any of these sources and have difficulty paying the costs, talk to the funeral director – they may agree to be paid in instalments. If paying for the funeral would cause financial problems, you may need to say that you are not willing or able to make the arrangements. In such a situation the local or health authority might have to take responsibility.

174

Sorting out the person's property and possessions

When someone dies, everything they own – their money, property and possessions – is called their estate. It may well be your responsibility to sort everything out.

Case study

Sarah said:

'Mum was the paperwork person. She paid all the bills and everything, so when she died Dad didn't know where anything was. I had to take on the paperwork, sorting out all the bills and so on. But I learned from this and I've now got all my finances sorted out so that, when anything happens to me, my children won't have to go through what I had to when Mum died.

'I'm contributing into two pension plans, so I'll be okay when I'm old and I feel I've got everything sorted. I've made a Will ... Mum didn't make a Will and we had to get someone in to find out what she'd got. I've written down who is to have what. I've got life insurance and personal accident insurance, too ... Mum didn't have any insurance, so we were left with all her debts to pay off. I will check it over every few years to make sure it's all still okay but I think it's all right. I've set up a good filing system so that my children will be able to find everything. Losing someone is bad enough without having all that to sort out afterwards. I had no time to grieve because I was too busy and that's taken its toll, I think.'

Sarah had difficulty sorting out her mother's estate because the paperwork was not all in one place or filed. She has learnt a lot from the experience and made sure that her children will not have the same difficulties. The matter of paying off debts can be complicated; although spouses are responsible for each other's debts, such as hire purchase or credit cards, others do not have to be paid by the relatives if the person's estate is insolvent. (See Chapter 4 for further information on legal and financial matters.)

Any bank accounts in the dead person's name only will be frozen until the formalities have been dealt with. Bank accounts in joint names should be transferred to the name of the other (surviving) account holder. If you had Power of Attorney or Enduring Power of Attorney for the person you cared for, because they were no longer able to deal with their own money and affairs, you must not continue to use their bank account or carry out any business on their behalf. This is because either Power stops being valid as soon as the person dies.

The Will

If the person who died has left a Will, this will indicate how they want their estate to be divided after their death. It will usually name executors (the people they want to deal with carrying out the instructions in the Will). People who receive money or property under the Will are called 'beneficiaries'.

The executor (or personal representative) will deal with sorting out the estate. If you are the personal representative, you should get some advice fairly quickly. A Citizens Advice Bureau should be able to help. If the Will is complicated, you may be advised to consult a solicitor, and the Citizens Advice Bureau can suggest local firms who deal with this kind of work. They can also advise you whether you might be eligible for help with paying the solicitor's fees. Getting professional advice early on can save a lot of problems later. You can, for example, make sure that any tax problems are sorted out, debts identified and paid, or arrears of benefit collected. Once these have been dealt with, the rest of the estate can be divided up according to the Will.

If the Will appoints a firm of solicitors either as executors or to act for the estate, all papers should be handed to them for them to obtain probate. However, if the Will does not appoint solicitors, the executor or personal representative can decide whether to engage solicitors to obtain probate. Ask the solicitors for a quotation regarding their charges.

If there is no Will to specify who is to receive anything from the estate, there are legal rules which have to be followed; the nearest relative will usually act as personal representative. A Citizens Advice Bureau adviser or a solicitor can explain these to you. Age Concern's Factsheet 14 *Dealing with someone's estate* also has useful information.

Personal belongings

If you are the executor or personal representative, you should ask all banks, building societies and other places where the person's money is held to freeze the accounts to prevent any misuse, and to inform you what the balance is in each account. You should collect all personal documents and list all assets, to enable you to assess the value of the person's estate and to obtain probate, if necessary, after which you should collect all assets and money owed to the person, pay debts (including income tax, if applicable) and then distribute the assets according to the Will or the rules of intestacy.

Personal documents such as pension books, passport, driving licence, cheque book and credit cards should be returned to the offices that issued them. If you need to send bank or credit cards through the post, cut the cards in two to prevent them from being misused if the letter goes astray. Make a note of all cheques written but not cashed, as these debts may need to be paid before funds are distributed.

Any equipment provided on loan (eg wheelchair, bath accessories or hearing aid) should also be returned to the organisations that issued them.

If the person was living in a care home, you may find that you have to remove personal belongings very quickly after the death so that the home can re-let the room. This can be very distressing for relatives but most care homes will try to deal with the situation as sensitively as possible. On the other hand, you may find that, under the contract with the home, you have to pay the care home for a few days or weeks after the person has died, in lieu of notice given when someone leaves voluntarily. This is normal practice but again it can be difficult for you.

Some people find it very distressing to sort through and dispose of the belongings of someone who has died. Perhaps it would help to do this with other family members or a close friend. You will be able to share your memories and are less likely to throw away small things that someone else might have treasured as a memento. Any items that are likely to be valuable can be separated out and sold separately, perhaps by auction. Charity shops are usually pleased to accept personal belongings for sale, and other charities may give them to families in need, either in the UK or abroad. If you really want to leave the task to someone else and are confident that there is nothing of financial or personal value, there are companies that specialise in clearing houses. They probably advertise in the local newspaper and/or are listed in the telephone directory.

Sorting out your own finances

If you have been the main carer for the person who has died, it is likely that your own financial situation will change considerably. Everyone's situation is different, so it is vital to get advice specific to you. You can get this from a Citizens Advice Bureau, Carers UK's CarersLine or the Benefits Enquiry line (listed in your local phone book).

The main areas you may need to look at include:

■ benefits and pensions;
■ housing.

We examine each of these areas to look at the possible consequences for you.

Benefits and pensions

There are many benefits and pensions that may be applicable to your particular situation, so you need specific advice from a benefits adviser. However, we can provide some general advice on the most common types of payment you might have been receiving, because it is important not to continue to collect benefits and pensions if your entitlement to them has ceased. If this happened, you would eventually have to pay back any over-payments.

Payment of Carers Allowance and the Carer Premium as part of a means-tested benefit can continue for eight weeks after the person has died.

If you are not receiving a retirement pension or Income Support, you need to sign on at the JobCentre as being available for work so that you can claim benefit (eg Jobseekers Allowance). If you are not well enough to work, you may be able to claim state benefit on the basis of incapacity for work instead.

If you get Income Support, you do not need to sign on for work for the first eight weeks as the benefit will continue to be paid and National Insurance credited for this period.

If you were married to the person you were caring for and you were both getting Retirement Pension, you may be able to get extra pension using your spouse's National Insurance contributions.

Housing

Housing problems sometimes arise for carers when the person they care for dies.

Home owners

If the property you live in was owned by the person who has died, it forms part of the estate and normally passes to the people named as beneficiaries in the Will. If you were not married to the person and not named as beneficiary, or there is no Will, you have no right to stay in the home; but get legal advice about this. If you are one of several beneficiaries, each will inherit a share of the property. In this case it may have to be sold unless you can afford to buy out the other beneficiaries.

If you were supported financially by the person who has died, you may be able to apply to the estate for some provision for your housing. However, this may be an expensive and lengthy business.

179

Council tenants

If the person who died was a council tenant, their spouse can normally inherit the tenancy and have the absolute right to stay in the property. An unmarried partner or other relative can usually inherit the tenancy if they have lived there for the last 12 months. However, they can be asked to move to a different property if the landlord needs it for other purposes. The landlord might consider the present property is too big for their needs, or it might be adapted for wheelchair use and the landlord might want to offer it to another disabled person. If this happens and you do not want to move, get specialist advice as soon as possible.

Private tenants

If the person who died was the tenant of a private landlord or housing association, usually only the spouse or opposite-sex partner can inherit the tenancy. However, some housing associations may allow other family members to inherit in certain circumstances.

If you have any worries about housing, get advice as soon as possible. Ask a Citizens Advice Bureau for help. It may be able to give you advice or refer you to a law centre or specialist housing advice service. Take along all the relevant documents, tenancy agreements, etc, so that the adviser can check exactly what your position is.

Case study

Peter said:

'The landlord's always been very supportive while Pat's been ill … I've lived here 30 years … and now she's in long-term care he's said to me that if I want to move into one of his other places I can. I don't go into her bed-sitting room now she's in hospital you see … I live in the rest of the house … but it's got too many memories for me. When Pat dies I'll want to make a fresh start.'

Your feelings

Now that we have looked at some of the things you have to deal with immediately when someone dies, let's take some time to review how you might be feeling at this difficult time.

Case study

Maria said:

'My mother died in hospital, so there were nurses we could ask about what we had to do, but you have this feeling like being in a tunnel or inside a bubble and everyone else is outside, and normal, and you just can't take in what they're saying, or concentrate on anything. When I think back now, it all seems a complete jumble. There's a lot to do in the first few days, and you feel like you're running round doing things all the time, but you can't remember exactly what you did when, or which bit of paper you took where. It's a bit like trying to find your way out of a maze when you've been hit over the head with a sledgehammer.'

Maria talked a bit about her feelings in the first few days, but everyone reacts differently. Some people feel overwhelmingly sad, others feel drained of emotion, perhaps dazed or numb or a muddled mix of feelings. Whatever your reaction, be assured that it is normal and natural. Give yourself time to get used to what has happened before leaping into action.

Whatever your feelings about the person you were caring for, their life has probably been very closely bound up with yours and their going will make a real difference to you.

Case study

Emily's mother died recently and left Emily with a feeling of emptiness.

'We were tied for all those years she lived with us. I thought I would appreciate the freedom, but I find I miss her a lot. It's a strange feeling, suddenly having so much time on my hands.'

People sometimes shrug off a death, saying: 'Oh, well, it was for the best.' But, while this may be true, it is important to allow yourself to be sad. The funeral, which is a formal public event, can be a very important moment in helping you and others to mourn.

Shock

Even if you have been prepared for some time for a death to happen, you are likely to feel shocked immediately afterwards. While this immediate shock will probably wear off quickly, the feeling of 'I can't believe it' can go on for longer. You may find you automatically carry on as though the person was still alive, buying their favourite food or expecting them to be there in their favourite chair. As the immediate shock of the death fades, you may find that the muddle of feelings starts to sort itself out.

Case study

Bill said:

'My wife had multiple sclerosis and died two years ago. Now I can start to look back further than the tough times we had over her last few years and remember all the happy times and mourn the lovely person she was.'

Guilt

Many aspects of caring can make you feel guilty. There always seems to be a nagging feeling that you could have done more.

Case study

Jean said:

'I looked after my dad when he had a stroke. After he died it was such a relief to be able to go out shopping without worrying that he would need me while I was out. Now I sometimes feel guilty because I enjoy the freedom and not having the responsibility any more.'

Just as you might have felt guilty while they were alive, you can feel guilty, as Jean did, after someone dies. You may feel guilty because you sometimes wished the person would die and now they have. All these feelings are very common among carers. The important thing to remember is that you did what you could. No one could ask you to do more than that. Now you can enjoy a freedom you didn't have before – try to see that as your right, not as something to feel guilty about. Guilt can be very destructive; if you are very troubled by it, it may be worth seeking some help from a counsellor.

Anger

Case study

Nancy said:

'I still sometimes feel resentful because I spent my hard-earned retirement looking after my mum and not going on that world cruise I had promised myself. When I hear people talking about what they are going to do when they retire, I say: "Don't wait. You never know what might happen."'

Like Nancy, you might have had to give up a lot to be a carer. It is very normal for carers to feel anger and resentment at their situation. Other people's lives can seem enviable and carefree compared with yours. When we feel angry we often take out the anger on someone or something else, and the anger may not go away just because the person has died.

Depression

Great changes in our lives can often cause depression. The death of someone close to you is very stressful and causes tremendous changes. Feelings of depression may not happen immediately, indeed you may get a rush of energy in the first few days and weeks. It may creep up on you a bit later when you realise that life has to go on. When familiar routines and activities disappear, you can feel very alone, even if at first it was a relief.

For most people, feelings of being down, tired and low get better by themselves, especially if you use some of the strategies suggested in Chapter 7. For a few people, however, depression becomes more serious. They may feel exhausted the whole time, have no energy, no appetite, sleep badly, burst into tears without any apparent reason and feel unable to cope with everyday life. If this happens to you, don't be afraid to ask for help, perhaps from your GP.

Who can help?

Usually relatives, friends and neighbours are the first and most immediate source of help, both in practical ways and in helping you come to terms with the death. They may be able to help with some of the arrangements and provide you with support. They may have known you both well and appreciate the situation you find yourself in. They may also share some of the feelings you are experiencing.

Case study

Sarah said:

'Don't be afraid to ask for help. Especially if you're an only child, you feel it is all your responsibility … everything's on your shoulders.

'Knowing that you're not the only one is so important. You're thinking … who can I talk to … who can I turn to?

'It was the GP who told me about Carers UK. She said there's this organisation that knows all about carers' rights and can put you in touch with other people. It was difficult to get anyone else to listen. She also told me about CRUSE, who help when you have been bereaved.'

When someone dies, those who were close often want to talk about them, as a way of remembering them and grieving for them. Friends and neighbours, however, may be reluctant to talk for fear of upsetting you or embarrassing themselves. You may have to tell them that it's OK to talk about the person who has died and that you want them to share their memories and sadness with you. People who care about you will want to be guided by you as to the best way they can help.

There is no right way of dealing with emotions. Listen to yourself and do what feels comfortable and helpful for you. Don't do what other people say you should do unless you really want to. Some people cope best on their own. Others find they are helped by talking about their feelings to someone else. Counsellors are trained to listen and help you untangle the things that are troubling you. One counsellor described the process as:

'unpacking the feelings and looking at them. Once you've looked at them, it is much easier to say: "Yes, I've felt that. I know why I felt that. There were good reasons for feeling that way. Now I can pack those feelings away and move on."'

Many organisations provide counselling, either generally or specifically for people who have been bereaved (eg CRUSE). Your GP may have a counsellor attached to the practice and may be able to refer you for counselling on the NHS. Contact details of CRUSE and the British Association for Counselling and Psychotherapy are given on pages 238 and 231.

Be assured that the immediate sadness and shock will fade. Other feelings will also become less intense as the weeks and months go by. As you pick up your life again, you will probably find that you are able to think about your time as a carer and the person you cared for in a calmer, less painful way. You will move on and be able to make plans for the future. The sadness of the death may always be part of your emotional make-up but it will no longer be the first or only thought in your head.

Case study

Sarah said:

'It all started in about March 1999 with Dad getting jaundice. Mum was already housebound but Dad was managing to look after her with support from me just popping in two or three times a week. I was working full-time and living away from home with my partner at that stage, but when Dad went into hospital I had to move back and give up work to look after Mum.

'Dad had an operation in the local hospital to remove his gall bladder but there were complications and so they sent him up to London for more surgery. I visited him every other day while he was up in London … I don't drive, so that was all by public transport, which wasn't easy. What happened next was that, while Dad was in hospital, Mum developed breathing problems. At first they put her into the local cottage hospital for a couple of days to see if they could sort things out but she got worse so they transferred her to the main hospital. Well, she died 12 days later. I think she just gave up … lost the will to live.

'After Mum died, I had to go and tell Dad, which wasn't easy. I was really worried about leaving him there in hospital, as you hear so many stories … about couples dying within a few weeks of each other. I didn't want to lose him as well. I felt it was important to get him home into familiar surroundings.

'Although I've got new friends and new interests, things have changed a lot. I've had to cut back on everything … it's ages since I went out at a weekend and I've taken a huge drop in income. I was in quite a well-paid job before. Now I'm down to £150 to £200 a month if I work two days a week and get Attendance Allowance for Dad. I have certainly lost my independence … but I feel I'm doing what's important.

'My partner and I are still together and we've got a baby on the way now, so we're planning for the future. I'm going to carry on working part-time because I think I need that break to keep me sane. Then I'll have maternity leave, of course, but I want to go back.

'I've put my old career on hold, really. Three years ago I wanted to go back to that lifestyle but I've learnt there are more important things in life than money and status. When something like this happens, you wake up to what's really dear to your heart. There's food in the fridge and we can pay all the bills and my dad's as happy as Larry. I'm making him a granddad at last. "Not before time" he says!'

Key points

■ The GP who has been looking after the person who has died can confirm the death and issue a Medical Certificate of cause of death and a Formal Notice explaining how to register the death.

■ Deaths have to be registered with the Registrar – either direct or via your local Registrar – within five days in the area in which the death occurred (eight days in Scotland).

■ It may be helpful to wait a while before the funeral, to make sure the arrangements are exactly what you want and to give some notice to the people who want to be there.

■ When someone dies, everything they own – their money, property and possessions – is called their 'estate'.

■ If the person who died has left a Will, this will indicate how they want their estate to be divided after their death. It will usually name executors (the people they want to deal with the instructions in the Will). People who receive money or property under the Will are called 'beneficiaries'.

(Continued)

- If there is no Will to specify who is to receive anything from the estate, there are legal rules that have to be followed.

- If you have been the main carer for the person who has died, it is likely that your own financial situation will change considerably. Everyone's situation is different, so getting specific advice is vital.

- Housing problems sometimes arise for carers when the person they care for dies, so get some advice if this is likely to apply to you. Ask the Citizens Advice Bureau for help. It may be able to give you advice or refer you to a law centre or specialist housing advice service.

- Whatever your feelings about the person you were caring for, their life has probably been very closely bound up with yours and their going will make a real difference to you. Everyone reacts differently. Some people feel overwhelmingly sad, others feel drained of emotion, perhaps dazed or numb or a muddled mix of feelings. Whatever your reaction, be assured that it is normal and natural.

- There is no right way of dealing with emotions. Listen to yourself and do what feels comfortable and helpful for you.

- The immediate sadness and shock will eventually fade. Other feelings will also become less intense as the weeks and months go by. As you pick up your life again, you will probably find that you are able to think about your time as a carer and the person you cared for in a calmer, less painful way. You will move on and be able to make plans for the future. The sadness of the death may always be part of your emotional make-up but it will no longer be the first or only thought in your head.

Appendix
Some techniques for safer
handling*

*Adapted, with kind permission, from *Safer Handling of People in the Community*, by Sally Cassar, Joyce Cheney and Ron Steed, and published by BackCare. (Techniques that require more than one carer have been omitted.)

General principles of safer handling†

Being aware of the general principles of safer handling will help to reduce strain and damage to your spine. In this context, 'handling and moving' is when you help the person to help himself. 'Lifting' is when the person cannot help and all his weight is being taken by a hoist or by you.

Your main aim should always be to help the person move himself. Do not lift unless *absolutely* essential. If lifting is necessary, you should use a hoist. If a hoist is not available, get help to lift – even if you have to wait. **Never lift on your own**.

Ask the local physiotherapist or district nurse to show you how to handle the person correctly. If this is not possible, or if you would like a reminder, the following principles should help:

1   Never lift on your own, unless it is an emergency, for example a fire.

2   Know your own strength and ability, and get help if needed. Always assess what you are going to do before attempting to do it. Look at the risks

(Continued)

189

involved, and be sure to consider matters such as your own personal ability and how you are feeling. Next, consider the person's ability to help and whether he will co-operate. Finally, think about the surroundings – the room in which you are working and the equipment you have to help with the task. Take time to plan exactly what you are going to do. If you have help, plan the move together but decide who is going to control the move.

3   Make sure you have room to move, and that your way is clear of loose rugs, handbags, children's toys and pets. Watch out for telephone wires, and make sure that catheters are secure. Get the furniture or equipment in position; where a wheelchair is involved, make sure that the brakes are engaged.

4   Wear suitable clothing that allows free movement and suitable flat footwear.

5   Explain to the person exactly what you are going to do. Enlist his full co-operation and agree how much help he will give.

6   Always move the person towards you, not away from you.

7   Always keep the weight close to your body. You should be so close to the person that your bodies are touching. If the move is taking place on a bed, you can get closer by putting your nearside knee on the bed, next to the person's hip. You should get the person to move nearer to you before you start the move. Remember: the closer the weight, the lighter it seems.

8   Have available a sliding sheet, a handling sling and a handling belt as appropriate.

9   Good posture is essential. Hold your head up, avoid stooping and keep relaxed at all times. Check your posture by keeping this checklist in mind:

feet	keep them flat and apart, one foot pointing in the direction of the move
knees	keep relaxed
waist	never twist while lifting – move feet in small steps, keeping your feet in the line of the movement you are intending to make

(Continued)

back	do not stoop; maintain the curve
head and neck	keep in line with your back, not dropped forward
hands	use a firm and comfortable hold, with the whole hand.

10 Brace your abdominal muscles, low back muscles and pelvic floor muscles so that you feel your back and pelvis supported. If you breathe in and hold it as you are about to lift, this further braces the back, but do not breath-hold beyond your own comfortable limit.

11 Where possible, have working heights adjusted and secured to avoid having to stoop or stretch. This includes chairs, beds, toilets, tables and storage areas.

12 Move only a short distance at a time, or you will twist your body, strain your back and be off-balance. Several short moves are safer than one long one.

13 Whether moving with other carers or alone with the person, use rhythm and timing. Say out loud: 'Ready, Steady, GO'.

14 When moving, your feet should be hip width apart, one in front of the other, facing in the direction you will be moving. One foot should also be close to the person to take the strain at the beginning of the move.

15 Try to keep the person between your knees – not to one side or too far in front. Any heavy work performed with the spine bending forward or twisted to one side is a danger to your back.

†Reproduced, with kind permission, from *Carers' Guide*, published by BackCare.

If you are going to use equipment, always ensure that the manufacturer's written instructions are accessible and that you follow them. Where appropriate, before carrying out moving and handling tasks, make sure that the brakes and other safety features are in good working order and use them correctly. Whenever you are moving someone in or around the bed, you need to make sure that the bed is at a suitable working height to allow good posture and the natural curves of your

191

spine to be maintained and that the total combined weight of you and the person you are moving does not exceed the safe working load of the bed (you may need to check this with the manufacturer).

You will often give verbal commands when helping the person to move. Be sure to speak clearly so that he can hear and participate as much as possible.

Terminology and illustrations

For the purposes of this appendix, the techniques can be carried out by either a male or female carer within their individual capabilities and limitations. **If in doubt, don't do it!** Seek help and advice.

For simplicity only, we refer to the person as 'he' and the carer as 'she'. Ths carries over into the diagrams, as well.

When describing how the various techniques are to be carried out, we refer frequently to using the 'near' or 'far' hand or arm. When a carer has taken up position to begin a manoeuvre, her 'near' arm is the arm closest to the person; her other arm is referred to as her 'far' arm. The same description is used to identify the specific limbs of the person; for example, 'near' leg, 'far' arm, etc.

Techniques

Techniques are described for the following types of moves.

1 Standing
2 Walking
3 Moving in bed
4 Sitting to edge of bed
5 Transfers
6 A falling or fallen person
7 Getting up from the floor

1 Standing

Before you ask the person to stand, establish his strength, joint mobility and balance. He must be able to bear weight through both legs and have adequate strength to raise his body to a standing position. If his lower limb muscles are weak, equipment may be required to help him to stand.

1.1 Preparation for standing

■ Make sure the person has adequate strength in his legs (see above) and is willing to stand.

■ Fit the person's footwear securely, ensuring that the soles are non-slip.

■ Clear the area and prepare the destination.

■ Ensure that all walking aids are close at hand and ready for use.

■ Wherever possible, ask the person to push down on a stable surface (bed lever, chair arm) to help himself to stand rather than holding onto you.

■ Never let the person push or pull up on a walking aid designed solely for support when standing (eg a walking frame).

1.1.a Positioning prior to standing from chair/toilet/ commode/bed/etc

■ Ask the person to shuffle or rock on his bottom to the front of the chair. If assistance is required, follow the technique described in 8.4 (below), except that you move the person forwards instead of backwards on the seat.

■ Check that the person's feet are flat on the floor, 'hip distance' apart and not tucked under the chair. It may be helpful to have him position one foot slightly forward of the other.

■ Ask the person to lean forwards so that he has a 'nose over toes' position.

- If the person rocks gently forwards and backwards, this sometimes helps build momentum for the move.
- Ask the person to push himself up on the arms of the chair into a standing position. As he stands, ask him to look up and ahead, not at the floor.

1.2 Standing without assistance

Once the preparation is complete the person may only need verbal prompting to stand.

1.2.a Independent standing from a chair

- The chair height should be such that the person can sit down with his feet on the floor and thighs level, one foot slightly in front of the other, unless a footstool is required.
- The seat should be firm and the back rest should provide support. A 'lumbar cushion', which supports the lower (lumbar) region of the spine, placed in the back of the chair may offer additional support and will bring the person closer to the front of the chair.
- The arm rest should be well forward, at least to the level of the front of the chair. A padded arm rest (but not too soft) is more comfortable for the person to use for pushing up and helping him to stand.
- There should be space underneath the chair and at its sides if you are to help him to stand.
- Make sure that any footstool or walking aid is not in a hazardous position.
- Consider powered riser chairs and self-riser cushions to help the person to rise by himself.

1.2.b Sitting down

- Make sure that the person can feel the front of the chair on the back of one leg or one of his knees.
- Ask him to reach down and touch the arm rests.
- He should then lean forwards ('nose over toes').
- He bends his hips and knees, at the same time sticking his bottom out towards the back of the chair while sitting down.

1.2.c Independent standing from a bed with equipment

- The preparation is the same as independent standing from a chair.
- Hand blocks (see 3.5.c) may be useful in providing a more stable surface than the mattress.
- If you are present and the person is in a height-adjustable bed, you could raise the bed as he stands, thus facilitating the manoeuvre.

1.2.d Helping someone to stand using a standing prop

A standing prop could be used if the person: has difficulty rising to a standing position but can bear his own weight (weightbear), can control his trunk and upper body, has enough strength to pull himself up if holding onto something secure, is not confused and will follow simple instructions. A standing prop consists of a fixed or turning platform (turntable) on which the person places his feet, and often a knee plate joined to a height-adjustable handlebar (see Figure A1). (If you buy or are lent any piece of equipment, you must ask for training in how to use it.)

Do not allow the person to use walking aids to help him to stand; they are designed to help with walking and can be unstable if used to stand up.

1.2.e Helping to stand using a standing hoist

A standing hoist could be used if the person has difficulty rising to a standing position but can weightbear, has trunk and upper body control but not enough strength to pull himself up, is not confused and will follow simple instructions.

He should be able to hold onto the hoist arms while placing his feet on the foot-plate with his knees resting against the knee-plate. It is important to position the sling well down his back to prevent it from riding up under his armpits. As the hoist rises, it pulls him into a standing position. Once the sling is positioned, it raises the person. If the sling slips up despite careful positioning, it could be that the person is weightbearing insufficiently and a standing hoist is not suitable. Slippery clothing (nylon, satin, etc) may also cause the sling to slip upwards (Figure A1).

Figure A1 A small standing hoist

1.3 Standing with assistance

Several methods can be used if more than verbal prompting is required to help someone to stand. Before starting any of these manoeuvres, ensure the following:

- There is adequate access and space around the chair/seat to perform the techniques.
- Whenever possible, ask the person to push up on a stable surface rather than on you.
- You should stand at the person's side, facing in the direction of travel with your feet apart and knees slightly bent.
- You should be on the person's weaker side.

1.3.a Hand holds (Figures A2 and A3)

Some carers feel more in control if they take the person's hand. The hand hold should be a palm-to-palm grip with the carer standing close. Whether you interlock thumbs will depend on any medical condition the person may have (eg rheumatoid arthritis affecting the hands) and whether he lets go easily.

Figure A2 The palm-to-palm hold, with thumbs interlocking

Figure A3 The palm-to-palm hold, with the thumbs not interlocked

1.3.b Standing with assistance

Encourage the person to push on a stable surface rather than on you.

- He can shuffle or wiggle forwards to the front of the chair or you may help him forwards.
- You must always be close to him if you are providing physical assistance to stand.
- Ask him to lean forwards into the 'nose over toes' position.
- Your far arm holds his hand palm to palm (with/without thumbs hooked), with his forearm held level. (A palm-to-palm hold is not always possible and you may have to give support at his elbow (see Figure A5).

197

- Place your near arm round his (Figures A4 and A5).
- If possible, fit a handling-belt to improve your grip (Figures A4 and A5).

Figure A4 Helping the person to stand, using the palm-to-palm hold and a handling-belt

Figure A5 Helping the person to stand by supporting his elbow and using a handling-belt

- Ask him to gently push down on your palm as he stands up.
- If he tends not to let go of your hand, ask him to push down on the chair arm or on his knee instead.
- Transfer your weight from your back leg to the front leg and move with him as he stands, staying close all the time.
- Give clear commands of 'Ready ... Steady ... Stand' while simultaneously using gentle rocking motions.
- On the word 'Stand' during the forward-rocking phase, he gently pushes down on your palm or the chair arm as he stands. *Note* If he is putting a lot of weight on your palm, this could indicate that his legs are not strong enough to raise him to a stand. At this point, reassess whether it is really feasible to help him just by yourself.

Once he is in a standing position, give him his walking aid (eg walking frame) if he uses one. (You need to make sure that this is nearby before you begin the stand!)

Certain techniques must be avoided. These include techniques that require you to stand in front of the person, use his armpit(s) or grip his upper arm.

Standing with assistance in a restricted space

If space is restricted or there is limited access at the side of the seat and it is not possible to create more space, a handling-belt must be fitted. You adopt an upright stance in a slightly more forward position and grasp the belt at the side of the person rather than at the back. This is a useful technique if his foot needs to be stopped from slipping forwards or when standing from a bed. You will need to transfer your body weight sideways from your rear foot to your forward foot during this stand.

1.3.c Standing to sitting with assistance

The movement described in 1.3.b is used in reverse. It is important to make sure that the person can feel that the chair is in position. Where possible, ask him to reach down to the arm rests and lower himself to the seat. If you are helping him to sit (or stand), it is important that you are in an unobstructed position and can move freely with him to avoid any sudden jerky movements or reaching and twisting movements.

2 Walking

Before walking, consider the following points:

- Is the person able to weightbear and move his feet without needing you to push or pull him forwards in any way?
- Are both of you wearing appropriate footwear?
- Does he know where he is – especially if it is night time?
- Is the planned route clear and have you considered equipment (eg catheters) to be moved as well?

■ Have you made preparations for him if he might be unsteady on his feet (eg have a chair nearby him or on the route)?

■ Can you rule out any other considerations that might increase the stress of walking (eg an urgent need for the commode)?

If the answer is 'No' to any of the above, you should reconsider the safety of getting him to walk.

2.1 Walking without assistance

2.1.a Independent walking

You can use verbal prompting to encourage him to walk without the need for physical assistance.

2.1.b Independent but using walking aids

You can consider aids such as a walking stick, walking frame or crutches or the use of handrails.

■ The use of walking aids may reduce the person's need for your physical assistance.

■ Any walking aids should be the appropriate height for the person. This will usually have been determined by a physiotherapist or occupational therapist.

■ Consider safety features and make sure that they are fitted if appropriate (eg rubber ferrules fitted to the end of the stick).

Don't use walking aids to help a person to stand. Don't allow him to hold onto them or push up from a chair onto them. Instead help him to stand (see 1.3 on page 196) and then place the walking aid with him. (Exceptions to this may include the use of a tripod under guidance of a therapist.)

2.1.c Mechanical assistance

A variety of hoists and walking systems are available. Talk to an occupational therapist about these.

2.2 Walking with manual assistance

2.2.a Walking a person who is unpredictable

Unpredictability is a problem found frequently, for example, when caring for people who have dementia. As a result of the unpredictability associated with this condition, someone may walk unaided one day but the following day he may unexpectedly choose to sit on the floor. An unsafe and unnecessary method frequently used by some carers is to lead the person by the hand. If he decides to sit on the floor or suddenly changes direction, the carer can be dragged along. If he does not need support, don't hold and/or lead him.

If the person is comfortable with his helper – you – his anxiety may be less and he may be better able to co-operate. This will reduce the risks to you. Everyone has the right to take risks – including someone with dementia – so long as they do not put others at risk

A handling-belt is the preferred option for walking with manual assistance.

- The carer holds and positions as 1.3.b (page 197).
- If a handling-belt is appropriate, position it as in 1.3.b.
- If a handling-belt is inappropriate, place your near hand on the person's far hip.

3 Moving up in bed

3.1 Rolling in bed without assistance

3.1.a Independent rolling

Using verbal prompting, encourage the person to turn towards you and follow your instructions as given below:

- Turn his head in the direction of the roll.
- Move his near arm away from his side or lift and position his arm and hand onto the pillow or place his arm across his chest.
- He places his far hand across his chest or holds onto the edge of mattress/bed in the direction of roll.
- He bends his far knee.

■ He rolls/pulls himself onto his side by pushing on the foot furthest away from you.

3.1.b Using grab rails, bed rails, bed lever, etc

Using verbal prompting, encourage the person to turn towards you and follow your instructions as given below:

■ Turn his head in the direction of the turn.
■ Either move the arm closest to you away from his side or lift and position the arm and hand onto the pillow.
■ Pace the hand further away from you across his chest and he holds firmly onto the grab rail/bed lever.
■ He bends the knee furthest away from you.
■ He pulls/rolls himself onto the side nearest you and pushes on the foot further from you to assist.

3.2 Rolling in bed with assistance

Be sure that you are able to move the person without harming yourself.

■ Raise the bed to optimal working height for you. Position yourself on the same side of the bed as the direction of the roll.
■ Turn his head in the direction of the roll; then either move the arm closest to you away from his side or lift and position his arm and hand onto the pillow. After positioning your own knee on the bed to reduce stretching, place his far hand on his chest (see Figure A6).
■ Move down the bed, with your knee still on the bed to reduce stretching, and bend his far knee. Then move back up the bed, placing your knee on the bed level with his chest.
■ Place one hand behind his shoulder blade and the other on his hip (Figure A7) with your elbow resting on his bent knee if this is comfortable. (*Note* Do not use his bent knee as a lever.)

Say 'Ready, Steady, Roll' and, on the word 'Roll', turn him onto his side towards you as you transfer your weight backwards – removing your knee from the bed but making sure that you do not step away from the bed just yet. If you do so, he may feel that he is rolling onto the floor and resist during the final stages of the manoeuvre.

Figure A6 Person on his side with the near arm up on the pillow, the far arm across the chest and the far knee raised

Figure A7 Place one hand behind the person's shoulder and the other on his hip, removing your knee from the bed while turning him

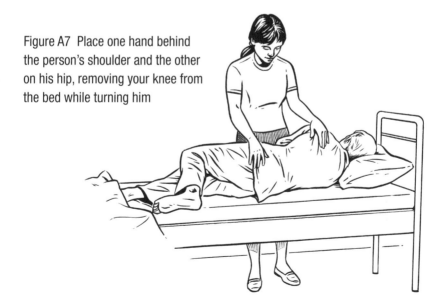

3.3 Sitting up in bed without assistance

3.3.a Verbal prompting

Using verbal prompting, you can encourage him to sit up in bed by rolling onto his side and then pushing himself up. This requires less effort than trying to encourage him to sit forwards from a lying-down position. Once he is in a sitting position, he can move back on his bottom. He can support himself when sitting by placing his hands on the bed just behind his hips. A rope ladder (see below), bed lever or grab rails may help.

3.3.b Rope ladder

Using a rope ladder fixed to the bottom of the bed (see Figure A8) may allow him to pull himself forwards. He 'walks' his hands up the ladder by pulling with each hand in turn.

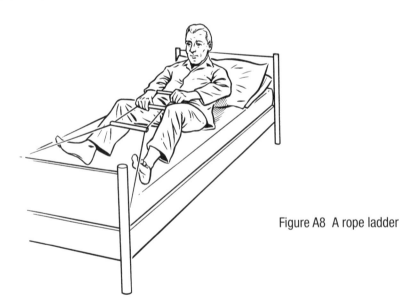

Figure A8 A rope ladder

3.3.c Bed lever or grab rail

Bed levers and grab rails firmly fixed in place allow him to obtain a firm grip on a secure object and pull himself up (see Figure A9).

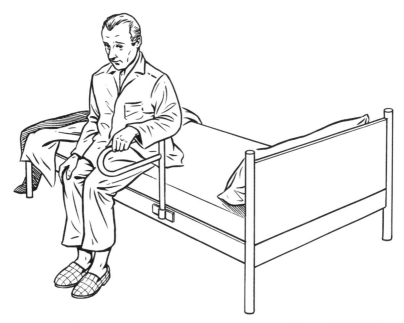

Figure A9 A bed lever

3.3.d Profiling beds, mattress inclinators and pillow lifters

The use of these items will reduce the need for you to help him to sit forward; he pushes buttons to operate and adjust the tilt of the bed, mattress and pillows. Profiling beds are described under section 3.5.a.

3.4 Sitting up in bed with assistance

For this to be carried out safely, he must be in a half-lying (or reclining) position and be able to provide most of the effort, you providing the least amount. The feasibility of this technique should be determined from an in-depth assessment by a professional.

■ If you don't have a mechanical device, place a soft handling sling behind his shoulder blades. This may be done by rolling him (see 3.2). You must hold the sling taut in both hands to prevent it from slipping; ideally, use a non-slip sling.

205

- Adjust the bed height to suit your height and to allow your supporting foot to be flat on the floor. Kneel on the bed on your nearside leg, with your knee at his hip/waist level.
- Rise up off your heel with your spine in a naturally upright position, thus creating a space between your heel and buttocks.
- For comfort, he slightly bends one knee.
- Make sure that the sling is taut and then ask him to put his chin onto his chest.
- Now say clearly 'Ready … Steady … Sit'.
- On the word 'Sit', transfer your body weight by sitting back onto your heels.
- As you sit back, your body weight is used to provide the minimal assistance needed to help him to sit forward.
- The end-result is you sitting down and him sitting up.

Caution Do not use the manual techniques described above (3.4), if he resists forward movements.

3.5 Moving up in bed

3.5.a Preventing slipping down the bed

1. Profiling beds The use of these beds greatly reduces the risk of injury to you because you need to do less moving and handling; at the same time, his independence is increased. Essentially, such beds can convert from a flat-bedded platform into a combination of positions. Profiling bed platforms come in two or three or four sections. The choice of the platform positions can help prevent a person from slipping down in the bed or decrease the number of times he needs to be repositioned. With the back-rest up there is a tendency for the person to slip down; raising the knee or foot section slightly will help reduce this.

Note Do **not** tilt the bed into a head-down position to prevent slipping: this can increase the blood pressure in someone who is lying down and may lead to medical problems for some people.

2. One-way glide This is an anti-slip low friction roller with Velcro strips inside to allow movement in only one direction. It will allow someone to slide up but not slip down. *Caution* The use of a one-way glide may not be recommended for people with fragile skin or poor circulation to the skin.

3. Careful positioning and choice of clothing If the person is initially correctly positioned either in bed or in a chair, the choice and positioning of clothing will help reduce the number of times you need to reposition him. For example, if you use sufficient pillows when positioning him sitting up in bed, they will give enough support to reduce slipping. Slipping will also be reduced if he wears comfortable cotton clothing rather than slippery fabrics such as nylon.

3.5.b Independent moving up the bed

1. Breaking down the move It is often useful to break down a simple move so that you can give clear instructions. The person will need reasonable strength in his arms and reasonable sitting balance to perform this move.

- He leans forward in bed.
- He bends one or both knees and digs his heels into the bed.
- He places closed fists on the bed just behind his hips.
- By simultaneously pushing into the bed with his heels and down into the bed with his closed fists, he can lever himself back up the bed.

2. Rocking and shuffling his bottom Just as it sounds, in this move he rocks onto one buttock while simultaneously moving the opposite buttock up the bed; then, maintaining momentum, he rocks to the other side while simultaneously moving the opposite buttock up the bed, and so on. This is repeated until he is in the desired position.

3.5.c Independent moving up the bed using handling aids

1. Using hand blocks The move is the same as 3.5.b(2) above but he uses hand blocks instead of closed fists. Hand blocks (Figure A10) provide a higher lift of his buttocks and make pushing down into the bed easier by providing a stable base. They are particularly useful on soft mattresses.

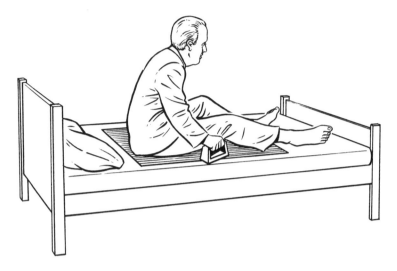

Figure A10 With one knee bent, the person moves by using hand blocks and a sliding device

2. Using sliding devices (low-friction rollers) You can place a sliding device under his buttocks to assist the movement backwards. If he cannot bend one or both legs to help in the move, a sliding device must be placed under the limb(s) to prevent his heels from dragging on the bed. Hand blocks (described above) may also be useful in combination with sliding devices.

3. By sitting to the edge of the bed Getting to the edge of the bed from a lying to sitting position is described in section 4.2.a. To get back up in the bed the person can:

- stand up, walk further up the bed and sit back down; or
- shuffle up the bed; or
- use a small sliding device (see the paragraph above) under his buttocks and slide further up the bed. *Note* If you use a sliding device, it must not hang over the bedside. Make sure that the person has adequate trunk control to prevent him from slipping off the bed.

3.5.d *Moving up the bed using a hoist*

If he is unable to contribute significantly towards movement back up the bed, and if assisted techniques are difficult, use a hoist (described in 7.5.a).

3.5.e *Move up the bed with assistance*

Backward slide up the bed

Using a sitting slide technique to move someone back up the bed is appropriate only if he is able to maintain a reasonable sitting balance. This technique should be used with caution as it relies on the person being able to participate by using his legs to help push himself up the bed. So he needs to be able to understand your instructions and commands during the move.

■ Place a sliding device under the person as in 3.5.c(2). Alternatively, he 'bridges' (ie bends his knees and raises his hips up off the bed, or leans side to side raising his buttocks) and you position the sliding device underneath him, along the length of the bed. The position of the sliding device is important. Some indicate where the person's hips should rest. For those that do not, it is easiest to position the device where the person should be at the end of the move; it can then be rolled back down under his hips and removed after he has been repositioned.

■ If necessary, he is then brought to a sitting position as in 3.4.

■ Position yourself just behind and to one side of his hip.

■ Place your near knee and lower leg on the bed, facing the foot of the bed and making sure that your knee is *under* the sliding device, not on top of it. Place your other foot firmly on the floor.

■ Sit up off your heel.

■ Hold each side of the sliding device with your hands.

■ Once in position, rise up off of your heel and hold the sliding device tautly in position.

■ Say clearly 'Ready … Steady … Slide' and, on the word 'Slide', sit back onto your heel as he simultaneously pushes up the bed by digging his heels into the mattress.

- More than one move up the bed may be needed. Take care not to overshoot and twist.
- Remove the sliding device, following the manufacturer's instructions.

> **Caution** If the person is obese, it is possible that the bed may tip as you sit back. Check the weight limit of the bed in the instructions accompanying it.

4 Sitting to the edge of the bed

4.1 Sitting to the edge of the bed without assistance

To achieve this the person must have strong arms and good sitting balance.

4.1.a Side-lying position

This method is described as for someone getting out of bed onto their left side.

- With his knees bent, the person should roll onto his left side and push his feet near to the edge of the bed.
- He places his right arm across his body and positions his right hand on the mattress at shoulder level, ready to use it to push.
- He simultaneously drops his legs over the side of the bed and, using his right hand, pushes himself sideways and upwards into a sitting position using his left elbow as a lever (see Figures A11 and A12).

4.2 Sitting to the edge of the bed with assistance

To achieve the moves described below the person needs strong arms and good sitting balance.

4.2.a Side-lying position with you assisting

This method is described as for someone getting out of bed onto their left side. If the bed height is adjustable, adjust it to allow you to provide some help without needing to stoop or twist.

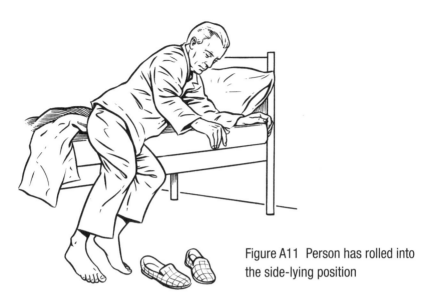

Figure A11 Person has rolled into the side-lying position

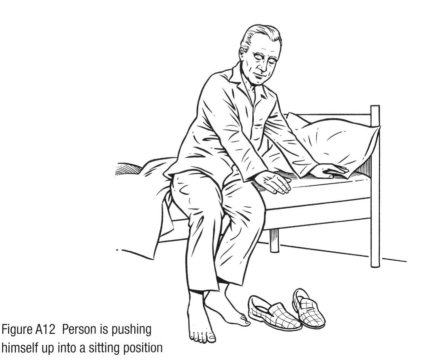

Figure A12 Person is pushing himself up into a sitting position

- With his knees bent, the person rolls onto his left side and pushes his feet near to the edge of the bed.
- He places his right arm across his body and positions his hand on the mattress near to the level of his chest and shoulder.
- He simultaneously drops his legs over the side of the bed and, using his right hand, pushes himself sideways and upwards into a sitting position using his left elbow as a lever, while you push up on his left shoulder (see Figure A13a).
- You help by holding both his shoulders (see Figure A13b).

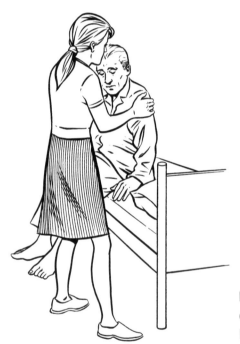

Figure A13 (a) The person uses his elbow to push himself up, with you helping by pushing on his shoulder.

The movement must be well co-ordinated. You must adopt a wide and stable base of foot support – stand with your feet hip distance apart, one foot slightly in front of the other and at an angle to each other (see Figure A13b) – and be able to transfer your weight from side to side in the process. If you place a soft handling sling under his calves, this will help reduce the need for you to stoop.

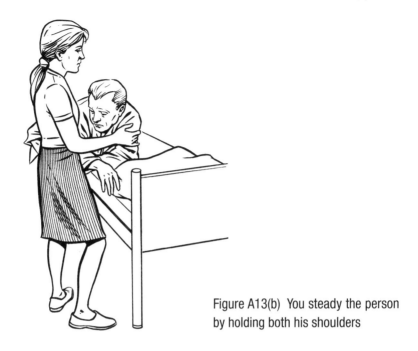

Figure A13(b) You steady the person by holding both his shoulders

> **Caution** On no account should you lift the whole or the bulk of the person's weight from a lying to a sitting position. If more assistance is required, use a mechanical aid such as a mattress inclinator.

4.2.b Assisting to sit to the edge of the bed with turning disc or sliding device

1. He has strong arms and good sitting balance As above (in 3.5), position a turning disc or sliding device under his buttocks to facilitate a swivel motion to bring him to a sitting position on the edge of the bed. You can also place a sliding device underneath his feet to facilitate movement of his legs to and from the edge of the bed.

2. He has sitting balance but cannot move his legs off the bed Position a low-friction roller under his bottom and a soft handling sling under his calves. Maintaining your back in a normal upright position, lift the handling sling while simultaneously turning him to the side of the bed. Once his legs are over the side, maintain your back in a normal upright position and bend your knees while lowering the handling sling under his calves.

3. He has sitting and standing balance but cannot move his legs back onto the bed You should consider using a mechanical system (eg powered leg lifters). However, if you cannot avoid having to lift his legs, use a reverse procedure as described in 4.2.b(2) on page 213.

5 Transfers

Examples of 'transfers' are moving from bed to commode, from wheel-chair to bed, from wheelchair to sofa.

5.1 Weightbearing transfers without assistance

5.1.a Independent (may need verbal prompting or encouragement)

With verbal prompting, he may be able to transfer independently.

- First, make sure that there are no obstacles in the way and that the destination can be reached easily.
- See 1.2, above.
- Once he is standing, he can step round to the chair/commode/ etc. This will be made easier if the distance to walk is as short as possible.

5.1.b Independent with aids

If he is unable to step round (once standing), consider the use of aids such as a turning plate (turntable) or bridging board. You can place a turning plate under the feet close to the destination – chair, toilet, etc. You can also use a bridging board. (Ask for specific advice from an occupational therapist about using turntables and bridging boards.)

5.2 Weightbearing transfers with assistance – chair to chair

5.2.a Transfer aids

Several transfer aids are available to help with standing and transferring someone. The following are described in more detail in the techniques below:

■ standing hoist;
■ mobile standing prop.

You should do this only if the person is able to fully weightbear and move with minimal assistance.

■ Use a handling-belt unless there is a particular rreason not to (eg he has a stoma from an abdominal operation).
■ Position furniture to allow you access to the side of the chair.
■ Position the destination chair (or commode, etc) close by.
■ Use the technique described in 1.3.b to bring him to a standing position and walk him round to the chair (commode, etc).
■ You must be able to stay at his side when he sits down unless he can let go and hold onto the arm of the chair to lower himself. You must maintain good posture as he sits down.
■ Reverse the procedure of 1.3.b to help him to sit down.

5.3 Non-weightbearing transfers without assistance

5.3.a Independent non-weightbearing transfer

■ Someone with good upper body strength may be able to shuffle sideways from one surface to another, independently. This can be done with or without a sliding board, and is extremely useful for someone who has had a limb amputated.
■ A turning plate under the person's foot or feet may ease the transfer movement.
■ You may help with a handling-belt.

5.3.b The person is unable to walk or stand but has good upper body strength

- Use a bridging board and a handling-belt if it is not contra-indicated.
- The person must have good sitting balance, good upper body strength, understand simple instructions and be able to participate in the move.
- Position the destination chair (or commode or toilet, etc) close by, with one end of the bridging board securely under the person's buttock nearest to the transfer surface.
- Position the other end of the bridging board securely on the chair (commode, toilet, etc) so that it bridges the gap. To prevent movement of the board when the receiving surface is uneven (eg a toilet seat), a non-slip netting can be rolled up under the board.
- A turning plate positioned under his feet may be useful in assisting movement.
- You stand in the gap behind him and between the two surfaces, and help him across the board by holding onto the handling-belt (moving with him to reach the destination). Make sure that you transfer your weight and do not twist your spine.
- If the move is more than you can achieve safely on your own, use a hoist.

As with all techniques, always be sure that it is feasible for you to undertake this on your own.

5.3.c Mechanical assistance

Hoists may be used for non-weightbearing transfers.

6 A falling or fallen person

There are several techniques in current practice and each one recognises that trying to stop a falling person is very unsafe and likely to lead to injury to you and possibly to the person himself. It is impossible to set out guidelines dealing with all situations. The following is intended as a guide only and is by no means exhaustive. The techniques described should be used only if you have been given specific training, and a moving and handling assessment has been completed for the person.

6.1 Assessment

Factors to be covered by assessment to establish the risk of falling include:

- A history of falling.
- The person's level of understanding of what is expected of him and how much is he able to co-operate.
- His physical and mental co-ordination (ie alert and not confused).
- Weightbearing abilities including balance, strength, medical condition and spasticity (or sudden muscle movement).
- Walking aids used, including walking frames, walking sticks, callipers, slippery footwear, prosthesis, etc.
- Environmental hazards such as loose carpets or rugs, electric fires or sharp objects, clothing, pets underfoot.
- Your capabilities, including your clothing and footwear.

6.2 Techniques

Falling person – you are in physical contact or delivering care at the time

There is no one safe way of dealing with him even if you are in close physical contact at the time. The following guidelines may be helpful:

- You may have more control if you position yourself behind him rather than in front.
- Have both your hands open while taking a step backwards but keeping close to him.
- You are likely to have more control holding his torso rather than his arms.
- Bend your knees and maintain a stable base to help protect your back while allowing him to slide to the floor.
- Support his head where possible.

- Allow him to fall rather than supporting him in an upright or slumped position.
- Do not take all of his weight.

When he is sitting on the floor and leaning against you, you may then step back and kneel down while protecting his head and maintaining your normal back position.

Then follow the recommendations in section 7, below.

6.3 Unsafe techniques

The following techniques are unsafe and should not be used:

- catching the falling person;
- trying to hold a collapsed person upright.

7 Helping the fallen person up from the floor

7.1 Being aware

Carers of people who walk or do standing transfers must always be aware of the possibility that they might fall. People receiving care should also be aware of such strategies so that they do not put pressure on carers to inappropriately help or lift them up from the floor. Unless the fallen person is in immediate and further danger, there is no need to hurry to get him up off the floor. He cannot fall any further, and acting without careful assessment could cause injury to both him and you.

7.1.a Assessment

If you find the person on the floor or ground and did not witness the event that brought him to the ground, first make sure that there are no dangers in approaching him (eg is there a live electrical lead touching him?). Make the area safe first and check that no further danger exists. Call for help. If the person is conscious, do not move him until help comes. If he is unconscious, the priority is to follow the recommended procedures for first aid and place him in the 'recovery position', as shown in Figure 3 on page 58. (First aid is beyond the remit of this book and you should seek advice about training from your GP or practice nurse.) When in doubt or if you are worried about the medical status of the person, call the GP, or dial 999. Do not attempt to lift or move the person without the appropriate equipment and before sufficient help has arrived unless there are overriding factors (fire/smoke, imminent collapse of the building, flooding/drowning, explosion, etc).

7.2 The uninjured conscious fallen person

7.2.a Independent transfer

It is useful to teach the instructions below to people who live alone and who regularly fall. It provides reassurance that they can get up by themselves and do not always have to wait for help to arrive.

- Stay calm and remain with the person, don't let him hurry to get up.
- Place a pillow under his head and wait until he feels ready to try to get up.
- Encourage him to bend up both knees (one at a time) and roll onto his side, and then push up into a side-sitting position.
- When he is ready, ask him to roll onto all fours.
- Bring a low stable chair or stool to his side.
- Encourage him to place his near hand on the seat and bring his near leg through so that he is able push up onto the near foot.
- Ask him to push down on his raised knee with his other hand.
- Encourage him to push down on the seat and through his foot while swinging his hips round to sit onto the seat.

You should never lift a fallen person up from the floor except in a life-threatening emergency, and then only after making absolutely sure that you do it as safely as possible for both of you.

7.3 Emergency lifting cushions/powered-air-raising devices

If the fallen person has sitting balance and trunk control and can stabilise himself using his arms, a powered-air-raising device can be used (with specific advice on its safe use). This has the benefit of being reasonably portable and can enable the person to get on or off the floor after a fall. Such devices often work on rechargeable power units, so they can be used anywhere. An example of when this device is helpful is for a wheelchair-dependent person who wishes to play with his children on the ground outdoors. In order to ensure stability, there needs to be some assistance from a second person when using the air-raising device.

There are emergency air-raising devices available for people who need back support (ie who lean back but have no sitting balance and do not fall to the left or right). Contact a Disabled Living Centre or Disabled Living Foundation for more information (contact details on page 242).

7.4 Restricted access to a fallen person

STOP! If you come across the person on the floor or ground and did not witness the event that brought them to the ground, first follow the guidance for approaching a fallen person (see section 7.1, on page 218). Wait until sufficient help has arrived.

7.5 Assisted transfers from the floor

7.5.a Hoist (sling or stretcher)

A hoist provides a safe method of mechanically lifting someone up from the floor. In most cases a fabric sling is sufficient; however, after a cardiac arrest (heart attack), a stretcher sling will be needed. Access slings that have little support should not be used to raise the person from the floor. If he has had a cardiac arrest, call the ambulance service on 999 and do not attempt to move him even after successful resuscitation.

Note Different makes of hoist use different approaches to moving a person off the floor and vary in their requirements for applying the brakes. Some recommend that you approach from the person's feet, some from the head or sideways with the person's knees raised for one of the hoist legs to fit under them. Others recommend either approach according to the circumstances. You should determine the manufacturer's recommendations and practise following their instructions before encountering a real situation.

7.5.b Transfers using a fabric sling with the hoist

Position the fabric sling in one of two ways. Either roll the person onto it or ask him to sit forwards, position the sling and then support him in a sitting position using a bean bag or the back of an upturned chair. If necessary, you can kneel with his head and shoulders resting on your knees. This gives him reassurance and can also make it easier to connect the sling to the hoist at his shoulders. You must avoid lifting his head and shoulders while you are in a kneeling position. Wait for help.

Once he is hoisted into a chair, it may be necessary to readjust the loops to achieve an upright sitting posture.

Always follow the manufacturers' instructions on the use of hoists and slings. Keep them to hand for when you need to check the guidance.

8 Repositioning in a chair

If people slump too much in a chair, there is a danger that they can slip to the floor. A lack of sitting balance or trunk control can cause this. It may be that the person's clothing is slippery or shiny, or he is simply slipping on the seating surface. It is sometimes difficult to position someone to the back of his chair correctly when using a hoist, and the sling is often removed before discovering that he is not positioned properly. You must not be tempted to lift him back yourself once the sling has been removed. There are several ways to position or reposition him so that he is sitting right at the back of the chair.

8.1 Preventing the slip

- Do not have slippery coverings on seats.
- Do not use anything that slopes downwards to the front of the chair, especially when he is wearing clothing made of a slippery fabric.
- Make sure that the seat is the right size, shape and depth for him and that he can sit supported with his feet on the floor or on a footstool or on the footplate or footrest.
- A one-way glide can be used to help prevent slipping. Some of these glides are padded with sheepskin or gel packs to provide some

protection against constant pressure, and some are available with handles. To reposition a one-way glide without handles, kneel down in front of the person and apply pressure through his knees to slide him back in the chair. One-way glides can also be useful to achieve a good seated position when using a hoist.

■ Lean him forward before sliding him back in the chair.

■ Take care not to lift him but to slide him.

■ Do not put a one-way glide on top of pressure-relieving seating.

Caution Use of a one-way glide may not be recommended for people with fragile skin or poor circulation to the skin.

8.1.a Repeated slipping

If there is repeated slipping even after following the steps above, it may be necessary to get him a chair that tilts back completely, or have a wedge on the seat to raise the front of the chair seat. If you use a wedge, be careful of pressure areas – the wedge shifts the weight of the person, concentrating it more under his buttocks.

8.2 Repositioning without assistance

8.2.a Verbal encouragement

■ Encourage him to bend both knees so that his feet are on the floor (as for sitting to standing).

■ Encourage him to lean forwards and then either:
   – stand up and sit down again with his buttocks as far back in the chair as possible, or
   – shuffle his buttocks back in the chair.

■ Alternatively, the chair can be brought closer to him if he is unable to step back.

■ If necessary, you can help him when he is standing as described in 1.3.b (page 199).

8.3 Repositioning using a standing hoist or sling hoist

If you are using a sling hoist for repositioning the person in a wheelchair with a tilt bar, the wheelchair can be tilted backwards as he is being lowered into it. This will facilitate positioning into the back of the wheelchair. (**Note** This method should not be used when repositioning someone in a large armchair.)

8.4 Repositioning with assistance without handling aids

- For unusual circumstances when the techniques described above are inappropriate or equipment is not available, it may be possible to assist the person to 'bottom walk' or 'hip hitch' back into the chair.
- You should be in front of him, in a high kneeling position (ie kneeling up, not sitting on your heels).
- Ask him to lean to one side and 'walk' or 'hip hitch' the opposite buttock backwards. Your role is to guide this manoeuvre towards the back of the chair either by helping him move his buttock or by gentle pressure through his knee towards the back of the chair.
- He then lifts the opposite buttock and leans to the other side; again you apply gentle pressure through his knee towards the back of the chair.
- He repeats the same manoeuvres on opposite hips/buttocks until he reaches the back of the chair.

9 Toileting

People often need help to use the toilet. It is useful to get help and advice from an occupational therapist who has a good working knowledge of useful equipment and adaptations in and around the toilet/bathroom area. An occupational therapist may consider some of the following:

- Fixed or fold-down grab rails.
- Toilet-seat raisers of varying heights.
- An automatic toilet that cleans and dries the person while he is sitting on the toilet. (This helps preserve independence, privacy and dignity,

223

and is welcomed by many people. It may not be as helpful for someone who has sudden muscle spasms, as the water jet may stimulate
muscle spasm.)

■ Raiser toilet seats to help the person to stand afterwards.

■ Bathroom or toilet adaptations, including repositioning of furniture
   and appliances to provide better access for the person and carer.

It is important that a detailed assessment is made before any equipment or adaptations are installed. All equipment or adaptations must be
properly fitted and the person must be taught how to use them. In
many cases, with the right equipment or adaptations, people can transfer independently to and from the toilet.

9.1 Adaptive clothing

It is often difficult to adjust someone's clothing for using the toilet. To
help, many people opt not to wear any undergarments and choose to
wear a soft, loose garment such as jogging trousers. Standard clothing can sometimes be adapted to facilitate use of the toilet. For
example:

■ For women, underwear is available with a drop-down edge at the
   front of the reinforced gusset secured with a Velcro strip. The Velcro
   strip must be positioned with the hooks facing away from the person
   so that the soft loop side can be secured by pressing it into place
   against the person.

■ Trousers with a drop-down edge are also available. This is useful if
   using a hand-held urinal with a tube leading to a toilet pan (and thus
   involves no need to transfer the person from a wheelchair).

■ Pants or trousers can be split at the back to preserve dignity at the
   front but allow easier access from behind.

■ An 'all-in-one' undergarment (teddy) with fastenings at the crotch or
   crotchless pants can provide easier access.

■ Dresses or skirts can be open-backed or wrap-over.

■ Zip flies for men can be replaced by Velcro that can provide quicker
   and easier access.

If standard undergarments are worn and the person is unable to stand, it may be necessary to ask him to rock from side to side or to lean over to one side at a time while you adjust clothing at the opposite side. This needs to be done in stages; you should be careful to adopt a posture that does not involve stooping and twisting. It is often necessary to kneel down next to him to adjust his clothing.

9.2 Transfers onto the toilet with assistance

For these transfers the techniques in 1.3, 5.1 and 5.2 are used. Whichever method is chosen (after an assessment of the capabilities and limitations of both of you), one important rule is:

Never support a person in a standing position while providing personal hygiene care or adjusting clothing at the same time.

This inevitably places you in a twisting and stooping posture while you are off balance and trying to support someone who, at that moment, is unstable.

Provided that a detailed assessment has established that it is safe for you to do so, you can provide help to someone who can stand and support his own weight by the following:

- a standing hoist;
- suitably placed grab rails (eg on the wall next to the toilet);
- walking aid (eg a walking frame in front of the person);
- rigid standing prop.

If the person can weightbear, all of these aids will enable full access for adjusting clothing or replacing pads.

9.2.a Person unable to weightbear

For a person who is unable to weightbear, you need to consider bridging board transfers. You will also need to consider the use of a sling lifting hoist. You can use an 'access' or 'toileting' sling to provide easy access for adjusting clothing while he is still in the sling. However, this type of sling does not give good support, so he will require good trunk control. If more support is required and a full sling is used, his clothing will need to be adjusted either after he has been transferred onto the toilet by rocking him side to side (similar to 5.3, page 215) or before the sling is put on (eg in bed). Cleaning may also have to take place back on the bed if a full sling is used. If a full sling is used, be careful to protect it from soiling on the return journey to the bed.

Remember You are not a grab rail nor a hoist and should not be used as one!

9.2.b Special considerations when helping someone to use the toilet

- Warn him not to push or pull on unstable surfaces such as sinks, taps and toilet roll holders, or to use you as a grab rail or hoist.
- To clean him while he is in a sitting or standing position, you must be sure that he is physically able and that there is enough space available.
- Cleaning could be done as follows:
  - encourage him to clean himself; gloves may be helpful if he has difficulty with co-ordination;
  - make sure he can reach the toilet paper and can tear a piece from the roll; if not, ready-folded sheets may be more useful or a device that automatically tears the paper;
  - asking him to lean from one side to the other or to lean forwards will provide access for you.
- Hoist him back on the bed onto a towel or disposable pad, then clean and re-dress him.
- If access to the toilet is restricted, transfer him onto a wheeled commode and either push this over a standard toilet or use it in an area where there is more space.
- It may be helpful to modify these transfers and positions if he has upper limb strength but problems with the use of lower limbs (eg both legs are paralysed or have been amputated). He could transfer onto the toilet forwards facing the cistern with his lower limbs or stumps astride the toilet pan.

- If he is using a bridging board, he may find it more difficult once clothing is removed. Sprinkling talcum powder onto the board will reduce friction but will increase the risk of the movement becoming less controlled and of him slipping off the board; this is, therefore, not recommended. An incontinence pad, plastic side up, may also help reduce the friction between his skin and the board, but the safest method is to adjust clothing once he is on the toilet.

- It is important to follow safety and hygiene procedures when helping him to use the toilet. Gloves and aprons should be used and care taken when emptying commodes. Regular emptying of the pan will prevent the need to lift a heavy, unstable load. To avoid spilling the contents when emptying a chemical commode, don't carry full pans over long distances or up and down stairs. Take care to observe basic handling principles when lifting and replacing chemical commodes. Deal with any spillages safely and hygienically.

10 Special situations

Special situations are too many and varied to be able to give individual guidance. Each situation must be judged on its own merits following a full assessment.

In all special situations the following approach is recommended:

- **Assess** Don't just rush headlong into the situation; look at all the circumstances surrounding it. Based on the assessment you should then:

- **Plan** what you intend to do and the things that must be done first to reduce the risks to the lowest level reasonably practicable. Then follow the guide of:

- **Minimal handling** You physically move him *only* if, based on your assessment, no other method is appropriate.

Details of all the equipment mentioned and how to use it is in *Safer Handling of People in the Community*, the book from which this extract is adapted.

Useful addresses

Not all the organisations listed here have been mentioned in the text. They are included, though, in case you might find them useful. For information about other, self-help organisations, ask at your local library for a directory such as *Charity Choice* (published by Waterlow Professional Publishing) or *Voluntary Agencies Directory* (published by the National Council for Voluntary Organisations).

Action on Elder Abuse
Astral House
1268 London Road
London SW16 4ER
Tel: 020 8765 7000
Fax: 020 8679 4074
Elder Abuse Response: 0808 808 8141 (10am–4.30pm, weekdays)
Email: enquiries@elderabuse.org.uk
Website:www.elderabuse.org.uk
Aims to prevent abuse of older people by raising awareness, education, promoting research and the collection and dissemination of information.

Age Concern
see page 263

Alcohol Concern
Waterbridge House
32–36 Loman Street
London SE1 0EE
Tel: 020 7928 7377
Fax: 020 7928 4644
Email: contact@alcoholconcern.org.uk
Website: www.alcoholconcern.org.uk
Has a wide range of information and can put people worried about their own or a relative's drinking in touch with a local agency.

Alzheimer Scotland – Action on Dementia
22 Drumsheugh Gardens
Edinburgh EH3 7RN
Helpline (24-hour): 0808 808 3000
Email: alzheimerscotland@alzscot.org
Website: www.alzscot.org.uk
Information, support and advice for people with dementia and their carers in Scotland.

Alzheimer's Society
Gordon House
10 Greencoat Place
London SW1P 1PH
Helpline: 0845 3000 336
Tel: 020 7306 0606
Fax: 020 7306 0808
Email: info@alzheimers.org.uk
Website: www.alzheimers.org.uk
Information, support and advice about caring for someone with Alzheimer's disease.

Arthritis Care
18 Stephenson Way
London NW1 2HD
Tel: 020 7380 6500
Helpline: 0808 800 4050 (12pm–4pm, Mon–Fri)
Fax: 020 7380 6505
Website: www.arthritiscare.org.uk
Publications (including *Arthritis News*): 0845 600 6868
Provides information, support, training, fun and social contact. The first port of call for anyone with arthritis. There are many smaller organisations for particular types of arthritis – Arthritis Care's helpline can provide details.

Association of Charity Officers
Unicorn House
Station Close
Potters Bar
Hertfordshire EN6 3JW

229

Tel: 01707 651777
Fax: 01707 660477
Email: info@aco.uk.net
Website: www.aco.uk.net
Over 200 member funds, including some that run residential and nursing homes for professional, commercial and occupational groups: the Occupational Benevolent Funds Alliance. If you need financial help from a charity fund, contact the Association, giving details of your family background and career pattern. The Association can signpost enquirers to funds that might be able to help them.

Association of Reflexologists
27 Old Gloucester Street
London WC1N 3XX
Tel: 0870 567 3320
Fax: 01989 567676
Email: info@aor.org.uk
Website: www.aor.org.uk
The largest independent organisation of reflexologists.

BackCare (formerly the Back Pain Association)
16 Elmtree Road
Teddington
Middlesex TW11 8ST
Tel: 020 8977 5474
Fax 020 8943 5318
Email: website@backcare.org.uk
Website: www.backcare.org.uk
The national association for healthy backs.

Benefits Enquiry Line for people with disabilities
Freephone: 0800 88 22 00 (8.30am–6.30pm, weekdays)
N Ireland: 0800 220 674
Textphone: 0800 243 355
State benefits information line for sick or disabled people and their carers.

British Acupuncture Council
63 Jeddo Road
London W12 9HQ

Tel: 020 8735 0400
Fax: 020 8735 0404
Email: info@acupuncture.org.uk
Website: www.acupuncture.org.uk
Regulatory body of acupuncturists.

British Association for Counselling and Psychotherapy
35–37 Albert Street
Rugby
Warwickshire CV21 2SG
Tel/Textphone: 0870 443 5252
Fax: 0870 443 5161
Email: bacp@bacp.co.uk
Website: www.bacp.co.uk
Publishes a directory of counsellors in the UK. Send an A5 sae for information.

British Chiropractic Association
Blagrave House
17 Blagrave Street
Reading RG1 1QB
Tel: 0118 950 5950
Fax: 0118 958 8946
Website: www.chiropractic-uk.co.uk
Regulatory body of chiropractors. Offers information about chiropractic and your nearest fully qualified BCA chiropractor.

British Federation of Care Providers
32 Shrewsbury Road
Craven Arms
Salop SY7 9PY
Tel: 01588 673 493
Fax: 01588 672 585
Website: www.bfcp.org.uk
Members must meet the standards of care set by the Federation. Can provide lists of homes; it also produces a useful checklist of questions to ask, called 'How to choose a good care home'.

British Heart Foundation

14 Fitzhardinge Street
London W1H 6DH
Tel: 020 7935 0185
Helpline: 08450 708 070
Publications ordeline: 01604 640016
Website: www.bhf.org.uk
Information about all aspects of heart disease. Heartstart UK arranges training in emergency life-saving techniques (tel: 020 7487 7110).

British Homeopathic Association (incorporating the Homoeopathic Trust)

29 Park Street West
Luton LU1 3BE
Tel: 0870 444 3950
Fax: 0870 444 3960
Email: info@trusthomeopathy.org
Website: www.trusthomeopathy.org
For information about homoeopathy and names of practitioners in your area.

British Institute of Funeral Directors

140 Leamington Road
Coventry CV3 6JY
Tel: 024766 97160
Fax: 024766 97159
Email: enquiries@bifd.org.uk
Website: www.bifd.org.uk
Information about arranging a funeral, including pre-paid plans, and about member funeral directors in your area.

British Lung Foundation

73–75 Goswell Streeet
London EC1V 7ER
Tel: 020 7688 5555
Fax: 020 7688 5556
Email: enquiries@blf-uk.org
Website: www.britishlungfoundation.com
Information about all aspects of lung disease and suitable gentle exercises for breathing control.

British Red Cross Society
9 Grosvenor Crescent
London SW1X 7EJ
Tel: 020 7235 5454
Fax 020 7245 6315
Website: www.redcross.org.uk
Services mainly provided by volunteers and available from local centres, including transport and escort, medical equipment loan, emergency response, fire victims support, domiciliary care, Home from Hospital schemes and first aid. Copies of the catalogue of aids to buy, The Ability Mail Order, available by telephoning 0116 270 1462.

British Telecom (BT)
For a free copy of the BT guide for people who are disabled or elderly, dial freephone 0800 91 95 91 to contact the BT Age and Disability Adviser.

Cancer BACUP
3 Bath Place
Rivington Street
London EC2A 3JR
Tel: 020 7696 9003
Helpline: 0800 800 1234
Fax: 020 7696 9002
Email: info@cancerbacup.org
Website: www.cancerbacup.org.uk
Europe's leading cancer information service, with over 4,500 pages of up-to-date cancer information, practical advice and support for people with cancer and their families and carers.

Cancerline
see Macmillan Cancer Relief

Care and Repair England Ltd
3rd Floor
Bridgford House
Pavilion Road
West Bridgford
Nottingham NG2 5GJ

Tel: 0115 982 1527
Fax: 0115 982 1529
Email: info@careandrepair-england.org.uk
A charity set up to improve the housing and living conditions of older people and disabled people. Routine enquiries should be addressed to Catriona Saxton, Company Administrator.

Care and Repair Cymru

Norbury House
Norbury Road
Cardiff CF5 3AS
Tel: 029 2057 6286
A charity set up to improve the housing and living conditions of older people and disabled people in Wales.

Care and Repair Scotland

236 Clyde Street
Glasgow G1 4JH
Tel: 0141 221 9879
A charity set up to improve the housing and living conditions of older people and disabled people in Scotland.

Carers UK

see page 262

Centre for Accessible Environments

60 Gainsford Street
London SE1 2NY
Tel/Textphone: 020 7357 8182
Fax: 020 7357 8183
Email: info@cae.org.uk
Website: www.cae.org.uk
Gives advice on accessible design for buildings.

Charity Search

25 Portview Road
Avonmouth
Bristol BS11 9LD

Tel: 0117 982 4060 (9am–3pm, Mon–Thur)
Fax: 0117 982 2846
Helps link older people with charities that may provide grants to individuals.
Applications in writing are preferred.

Chartered Society of Physiotherapy

14 Bedford Row
London WC1R 4ED
Tel: 020 7306 6666
Fax: 020 7306 6611
Website: www.csp.org.uk
For chartered physiotherapists in your area.

Chest, Heart and Stroke Association

21 Dublin Road
Belfast BT2 7HR
Tel: 028 9032 0184
Advice Helpline: 08457 697299
Fax: 029 9033 3487
Email: mail@nichsa.com
Website: www.nichsa.com
Promotes the prevention and alleviation of chest, heart and stroke-related
illnesses, in Northern Ireland.

Chest, Heart and Stroke Scotland

65 North Castle Street
Edinburgh EH2 3LT
Tel: 0131 225 6963 (9am–4.30pm, Mon–Fri)
Helpline: 0845 077 6000
Fax: 0131 225 6313
Email: admin@chss.org.uk
Website: www.chss.org.uk
Aims to improve the quality of life for people in Scotland affected by chest,
heart and stroke illness, through medical research, advice and informa-
tion, and support in the community.

Choice magazine
Choice Publising Ltd
1st Floor
2 King Street
Peterborough PE1 1LT
Tel: 01733 555123
Published monthly. To advertise for a companion.

Citizens Advice Bureau
Listed in local telephone directories or in *Yellow Pages* under 'Social Service and Welfare Organisations'. (Other local advice centres on any subject may also be listed.)
For advice on legal, financial and consumer matters. A good place to turn to if you don't know where to go for help or advice on any subject.

Commission for Healthcare Audit and Inspection
Website: www.chai.org.uk

Commission for Social Care Inspection
see under Department of Health.

Community Transport Association
Highbank
Halton Street
Hyde
Cheshire SK14 2NY
Tel: 0870 774 3586
Advice Line: 0845 130 6195
Fax: 0870 774 3581
Website: www.communitytransport.com
Services to benefit providers of transport for people with mobility problems.

Continence Foundation
307 Hatton Square
16 Baldwin Gardens
London EC1N 7RJ
Tel: 020 7404 6875
Helpline: 0845 345 0165 (nurse available 9.30am–12.30pm, Mon–Fri)
Fax: 020 7404 6876

Email: continence.foundation@dialpipex.com
Website: www.continence-foundation.org.uk
Advice and information about whom to contact with urinary/bowel
incontinence problems.

Council for Voluntary Service (CVS)
see National Association of Councils for Voluntary Service

Counsel and Care
Lower Ground Floor
Twyman House
16 Bonny Street
London NW1 9PG
Tel: 020 7241 8555 (admin)
Advice Line: 0845 300 7585 (10am–1pm, Mon–Fri)
Fax: 020 7267 6877
Email: advice@counselandcare.org.uk
Website: www.counselandcare.org.uk
Advice on remaining at home or about care homes.

Court of Protection
see Public Guardianship Office for England and Wales; Office of Care and
Protection for Northern Ireland; and Office of the Public Guardian for Scotland

Crossroads – Caring for Carers
10 Regent Place
Rugby
Warwickshire CV21 2PN
Tel: 01788 573653
  Scotland: 01412 263793
  Wales: 029 2022 2282
Helpline: 0845 450 0350
Fax: 01788 565498
Email: communications@crossroads.org.uk
Website: www.crossroads.org.uk
Has nearly 200 schemes across England and Wales providing practical
support to carers in their homes.

Cruse Bereavement Care
Cruse House
126 Sheen Road
Richmond
Surrey TW9 1UR
Tel: 020 8940 4818
Fax: 020 8940 7638
Bereavement line: 0845 758 5565
Helpline: 0870 167 1677 (9.30am–5pm, weekdays) 24-hour electronic
message
A counselling and advice service for those bereaved by death throughout the UK. Gives advice, information and practical support, in addition to personal and confidential help backed by a wide range of publications and leaflets.

CSV Volunteer Programme
237 Pentonville Road
London N1 9NJ
Tel: 020 7278 6601
Fax: 020 7833 0149
Email: information@csv.org.uk
Website: www.csv.org.uk
A national organisation that places full- and part-time volunteers to help individuals manage their social, practical, work and personal care needs. CSV volunteers need accommodation, food, a weekly allowance and travel expenses. There is a one-off charge to CSV plus an annual fee.

CSV Scotland
Wellgate House
200 Cowgate
Edinburgh EH1 1NQ
Tel: 0131 622 7766
Fax: 0131 622 7755
Email: scotinfo@csv.org.uk

CSV Wales
CSV House
Williams Way
Cardiff CF10 5DY

Tel: 029 2041 5717
Fax: 029 2041 5747
Email: csvcymru@csv.org.uk

Department of Health
PO Box 777
London SE1 6XH
Tel: 020 7210 4850
Textphone: 020 7210 5025
Health Literature Line: 0800 555 777
Fax: 01623 724 524
Email: doh@prolog.uk.com
Website: www.doh.gov.uk
Produces literature about health issues, available via the Health Literature Line.
See also www.doh.gov.uk/nhscharges for information about prescription
charges and prepayment certificates, including the application form FP95;
and ww.doh.gov.uk/csci for information on the Commission for Social
Care Inspection.

Department for Work and Pensions
Benefits Enquiry Line: 0800 88 22 00
Tel: 020 7712 2171
Textphone 0800 24 33 55
Fax: 020 7712 2386
Website: www.dwp.gov.uk
Government department giving information about, and claim forms for, all
state benefits. Your local ofice will be listed in the telephone book.

Diabetes UK
10 Parkway
London NW1 7AA
Tel: 020 7424 1000
Careline: 0845 120 2960 (9am–5pm, Mon–Fri)
Fax: 020 7424 1001
Email: info@diabetes.org.uk
Website: www.diabetes.org.uk
Help for people with diabetes and their families; branches across the UK.

239

DIAL UK (Disablement Information and Advice Lines)
St Catherine's Hospital
Tickhill Road
Doncaster DN4 8QN
Tel/Textphone: 01302 310123
Fax: 01302 310404
Website: www.dialuk.org.uk
Information and advice network run by and for people with disabilities.
Can put you in touch with local contacts.

Disability Alliance
Universal House
88–94 Wentworth Street
London E1 7SA
Tel/Textphone: 020 7247 8776 (10am–4pm, Mon–Fri)
Rights advice line: 020 7247 8763 (2–4pm, Mon & Wed)
Fax: 020 7247 8765
Website: www.disabilityalliance.org
Campaigning for a better deal for people with disabilities; information
about benefits and publishes The Disability Rights Handbook.

Disability Law Service
39–45 Cavell Street
London E1 2BP
Tel: 020 7791 9800
Fax: 020 7791 9802
Email: advice@dls.org.uk
Website: ww.dls.org.uk
Free legal advice on benefits, community care, consumer and contract
law, education, employment and disability, and discrimination, for disabled
people and their carers throughout Britain.

Disability Sport England
N17 Studio, Unit 4G
784–788 High Road
London N17 0DA
Tel: 020 8801 4466

Fax: 020 8801 6644

Website: www.disabilitysport.org.uk

National events agency that encourages sport from local to national level.

Disability Wales

Wernddu Court

Caerphilly Business Park

Van Road

Caerphilly CF83 3ED

Tel: 029 2088 7325

Fax: 029 2088 8702

Email: info@dwac.demon.co.uk

Website: www.dwac.demon.co.uk

National association of disability groups working to promote the rights, recognition and support of all disabled people in Wales.

Disabled Drivers' Association

Ashwellthorpe Hall

Norwich NR16 IEX

Tel: 0870 770 3333

Fax: 01508 488173

Email: ddahq@aol.com

Website: www.dda.org.uk

Information and advice for disabled drivers.

Disabled Drivers' Motor Club

Cottingham Way

Thrapston

Northants NN14 4PL

Tel: 01832 734724

Fax: 01832 733816

Email: info@ddmc.org.uk

Website: www.ddmc.org.uk

Information and advice about mobility problems for disabled people, whether they are drivers or passengers.

Disabled Living Centres Council

Redbank House
4 St Chad's Street
Manchester M8 8QA
Tel: 0161 834 1044
Textphone: 0161 839 0885
Fax: 0161 839 0802
Email: dlcc@org.uk
Website: www.dlcc.org.uk
Can tell you where your nearest Disabled Living Centre is – where you can get free information and advice about disability aids and equipment.

Disabled Living Foundation

380–384 Harrow Road
London W9 2HU
Tel: 020 7289 6111
Textphone: 020 7432 8009
Helpline: 0845 130 9177 (10am–4pm, Mon–Fri)
Website: www.dlf.org.uk
National charity providing information about disability aids and equipment.

DVLA (Driver and Vehicle Licensing Agency)

Medical Branch
Longview Road
Morriston
Swansea SA99 1TU
Tel: 0870 240 0009
Fax: 01792 761100
Email: drivers.dvla@gtnet.gov.uk
Website: www.dvla.gov.uk
Information on eligibility to drive.

Elderly Accommodation Counsel

3rd Floor
89 Albert Embankment
London SE1 7TP
Helpline: 020 7820 1343
Fax: 020 7820 3970

Email: enquiries@e-a-c.demon.co.uk
Website: www.housingcare.org
National charity offering advice and information about all forms of accommodation for older people. Has a national register of accommodation in the voluntary and private sectors, suitable for older people.

Foundations – the National Co-ordinating Body for Home Improvement Agencies
Bleaklow House
Howard Town Mills
Glossop
Derbyshire SK13 8HT
Tel: 01457 891909
Fax: 01457 879361
Email: foundations@cel.co.uk
Website: www.foundations.uk.com
To find out whether there is a home improvement agency locally.

General Chiropractic Council
44 Wicklow Street
London WC1X 9HL
Tel: 020 7713 5155
Fax: 020 7713 5844
Email: enquiries@gcc-uk.org
Website: www.gcc-uk.org
The statutory body regulating practitioners of chiropractic.

General Osteopathic Council
Osteopathic House
176 Tower Bridge Road
London SE1 3LU
Tel: 020 7357 6655
Fax: 020 7357 0011
Email: info@osteopathy.org.uk
Website: www.osteopathy.org.uk
For advice on finding a registered osteopath.

Greater London Action on Disability (GLAD)
336 Brixton Road
London SW9 7AA
Tel: 020 7346 5800
Fax: 020 7346 8844
Email: info@glad.org.uk
Website: www.glad.org.uk
Information for disabled people in the London area.

Headway (The Brain Injury Association)
4 King Edward Court
King Edward Street
Nottingham NG1 IEW
Tel: 0115 924 0800 (24-hour)
Textphone: 0115 950 7825
Fax: 0115 958 4446
Email: enquiries@headway.org.uk
Website: www.headway.org.uk
For people with a brain injury, and their carers.

Holiday Care
7th Floor, Sunley House
4 Bedford Park
Croydon CR0 2AP
Tel: 0845 124 9974
Textphone: 0845 124 9976
Helpline: 0845 124 9971
Fax: 0845 124 9972
Email: info@holidaycare.org
Website: www.holidaycare.org.uk
Information and advice about holidays for older or disabled people and their carers. Has a database of respite care facilities in the UK.

Help the Hospices
Hospice House
34 Britannia Street
London WC1X 9JG

Tel: 0870 903 3903
Fax: 020 7278 1021
Email: info@hospiceinformation.info
Website: www.hospiceinformation.info
A partnership between St Christopher's Hospice, London, and Help the Hospices. It offers an enquiry service to the public and professionals, and its publications include UK and International Directories of Hospice and Palliative Care.

Huntington's Disease Association
108 Battersea High Street
London SW11 3HP
Tel: 020 7223 7000
Website: www.hda.org.uk
Information, advice and local branches for carers of people with Huntington's disease (Huntington's chorea).

Independent Living (1993) Fund
PO Box 7525
Nottingham NG2 4ZT
Tel: 0845 601 8815
Fax: 0115 945 0948
May provide top-up funding to severely disabled people. Applicants must already be receiving the highest Care Allowance and at least £200 care package from social services. Referral is via social services. Applications must be made before the age of 66.

Institute for Complementary Medicine
PO Box 194
London SE16 7QZ
Tel: 020 7237 5165 (10am–3pm, weekdays)
Fax: 020 7237 5175
Email: info@icmedicine.co.uk
Website: www.icmedicine.co.uk
Information and advice about complementary therapy. Please send self-addressed envelope.

Jewish Care
Stuart Young House
221 Golders Green Road
London NW11 9DQ
Tel: 020 8922 2000
Fax: 020 8922 2585
Email: info@jcare.org
Social care, personal support and care homes for Jewish people in the UK.

The Lady magazine
39–40 Bedford Street
London WC2E 9ER
Tel: 020 7379 4717
To advertise for a live-in companion.

Leonard Cheshire
30 Millbank
London SW1P 4QD
Tel: 020 7802 8200
Fax: 020 7802 8250
Email: info@london.leonard-cheshire.org.uk
Website: www.leonard-cheshire.org.uk
Leading charity provider of services for disabled people in the UK.

Local government ombudsmen
Helplines: 0845 602 1983 (England); 01656 661 325 (Wales);
0870 011 5378 (Scotland); Freephone 0800 343424 (N Ireland)
Websites: www.lgo.org.uk (England); www.obwdsman-cymru.org (Wales);
www.scottishombudsman.org.uk (Scotland); www.ni-ombudsman.org.uk
(N Ireland)
Local government ombudsmen investigate complaints of injustice about local authorities and some other bodies. There are three for England, one for Wales, one for Scotland and one for N Ireland.

Macmillan Cancer Relief
89 Albert Embankment
London SE1 7UQ

Tel: 020 8563 9800

Helplines: 0808 808 2020

0800 808 0121 for people who are deaf or hard of hearing

Fax: 020 8563 9640

Email: cancerline@macmillan.org.uk

Website: www.macmillan.org.uk

Information about cancer services. Funds NHS Macmillan nurses for home care as well as hospital and hospice support.

MAVIS (Mobility Advice and Vehicle Information Service)

Department of Transport

Crowthorne Business Estate

Old Wokingham Road

Crowthorne

Berkshire RG45 6XD

Tel: 01344 661000

Fax: 01344 661066

Email: mavis@dft/gsi.gov.uk

Website: www.mobility-unit.dft.gov.uk

Driving assessments and advice for people with mobility problems.

MIND (National Association for Mental Health)

15–19 Broadway

London E15 4BQ

Tel: 020 8519 2122

InfoLine: 08457 660 163 (9.15am–5.15pm, Mon–Fri)

London Helpline: 020 8522 1728

Publications: 020 8221 9666

Fax: 020 8522 1725

Email: contact@mind.org.uk

Website: www.mind.org.uk

Information, support and publications about all aspects of mental illness, depression, etc.

Motability
Goodman House
Station Approach
Harlow
Essex CM20 2ET
Tel: 01279 635999 (admin)
Textphone: 01279 632213
Helpline: 08454 564 566 (8.45am–5.15pm, Mon–Fri)
Fax: 01279 632000
Website: www.motability.co.uk
Advises people with disabilities about powered wheelchairs, scooters, and new and used cars, how to adapt them to their needs and how to obtain funding via the Mobility Scheme.

National Association of Councils for Voluntary Service (NACVS)
Arundel Court
177 Arundel Street
Sheffield S1 2NU
Tel: 0114 278 6636
Fax: 0114 278 7004
Email: nacvs@nacvs.org.uk
Website: www.nacvs.org.uk
Promotes and supports the work of Councils for Voluntary Service. Or look in your telephone directory to see if there is a local CVS.

National Centre for Disabled Persons (including **Disabled Parents Network**)
Unit F9
89–93 Fonthill Road
London N4 3JH
Helpline: 0870 241 0450
Textphone: 0800 018 9949
Fax: 020 7263 6399
Email: supportworker@disabledparentsnetwork.org.uk
Website: www.disabledparentsnetwork.org.uk
Peer support, advocacy and membership.

National Centre for Independent Living

250 Kennington Lane
London SE11 5RD`
Tel: 020 7587 1663
Textphone: 020 7587 1177
Fax: 020 7582 2469
Email: ncil@ncil.org.uk
Website: www.ncil.org.uk
Provides advice on independent living and direct payments, and details of your local Centre for Independent Living.

NHS Direct

Tel: 0845 46 47
Website: www.nhsdirect.nhs.uk
First point of contact to find out about NHS services.

NHS24

Tel: 08454 24 24 24
Website: www.nhs24.com
The Scottish equivalent of NHS Direct, available in some areas of Scotland.

Office of Care and Protection (Northern Ireland)

Royal Courts of Justice
PO Box 410
Chichester Street
Belfast BT1 3JF
Tel: 028 9023 5111
Fax: 028 9032 2782
Email: officeofcare&protection@courtsni.gov.uk
If you need to take over the affairs of someone who is mentally incapable in Northern Ireland.

Office of the Public Guardian (OPG)

Hadrian House
Callendar Road
Falkirk FK1 1XR
Tel: 01324 678300
Information on Continuing Power of Attorney in Scotland.

Parkinson's Disease Society
215 Vauxhall Bridge Road
London SW1V 1EJ
Tel: 020 7931 8080
Helpline: 0808 800 0303 (9.30am–5.30pm, Mon–Fri)
Fax: 020 7931 9908
Email: enquiries@parkinsons.org.uk
Website: www.parkinsons.org.uk
Support and information for relatives and carers of someone with Parkinson's disease.

Patients Association
PO Box 935
Harrow
Middlesex HA1 3YJ
Tel: 020 8423 9111 (admin: 9am–5pm, weekdays)
Helpline: 0845 608 4455 (10am–4pm, Mon–Fri)
Fax: 020 8423 9119
Website: www.patients-association.com
Gives advice to patients and carers on patients' rights, complaints procedures and access to health services or appropriate self-help groups.

Pensions Advisory Service (OPAS)
11 Belgrave Road
London SW1V 1RB
Helpline: 0845 601 2923
Fax: 020 7233 8016
Email: enquiries@opas.org.uk
Website: www.opas.org.uk
A voluntary organisation that gives advice and information about occupational and personal pensions and helps sort out problems.

Princess Royal Trust for Carers
142 Minories
London EC3N 1LB
Tel: 020 7480 7788
Fax: 020 7481 4729
Email: info@carers.org

Website: www.carers.org
Aims to make it easier for carers to cope by providing information, support and practical help. Your phone book may list a local branch.

Public Guardianship Office

Archway Tower
2 Junction Road
London N19 5SZ
Tel: 020 7664 7300/7000
Enquiry Line: 0845 330 2900
Fax: 020 7911 7105
Website: www.guardianship.gov.uk
If you need to take over the affairs of someone who is mentally incapable in England or Wales.

RADAR (Royal Association for Disability and Rehabilitation)

12 City Forum
250 City Road
London EC1V 8AF
Tel: 020 7250 3222
Textphone: 020 7250 4119
Fax: 020 7250 0212
Email: radar@radar.org.uk
Website: www.radar.org.uk
Information about aids and mobility, holidays, sport and leisure for disabled people.

Ramblers' Association

2nd Floor, Camelford House
87–90 Albert Embankment
London SE1 7TW
Tel: 020 7339 8500
Fax: 020 7339 8501
Email: ramblers@london.ramblers.org.uk
Website: www.ramblers.org.uk
A membership organisation for walkers, which campaigns for access to the countryside.

251

Registered Nursing Homes Association
15 Highfield Road
Edgbaston
Birmingham B15 3DU
Tel: 0121 454 2511
Freephone: 0800 0740 194
Fax: 0121 454 0932
Email: info@rnha.co.uk
Website: www.rnha.co.uk
Information about registered nursing homes in your area, which meet the standards set by the Association.

Relate (formerly National Marriage Guidance Council)
Herbert Gray College
Little Church Street
Rugby
Warwickshire CV21 3AP
Tel: 01788 573241
Helpline: 0845 130 4010
Fax: 01788 535007
Email: enquiries@national.relate.org.uk
Website: www.relate.org.uk
Counselling and help with difficult relationships; many local branches.

Relatives and Residents Association
24 The Ivories
6–18 Northampton Street
London N1 2HY
Tel: 020 7359 8148
Helpline: 020 7359 8136 (10am–5pm, Mon–Fri)
Fax: 020 7226 6603
Email: advice@relres.org
Website: www.relres.org.uk
Support and advice for relatives of people in a care home or hospital long term.

REMAP
National Organiser
Hazeldene
Ightham
Sevenoaks
Kent TN15 9AD
Tel: 0845 1300 456
Fax: 0845 1300 789
Email: info@remap.org.uk
Website: www.remap.org.uk
For free customised aids and gadgets at no cost to the recipient.

Rethink (formerly **National Schizophrenia Fellowship**)
30 Tabernacle Street
London EC2A 4DD
Tel: 020 7330 9100/9001
Membership Line: 0845 4560 455
National Advice Line: 020 8974 6814 (10am–3pm, Mon, Wed, Fri;
10am–1pm, Tue, Thu)
Fax: 020 7330 9102
Email: info.london@rethink.org
Website: www.rethink.org
Working together to help everyone affected by severe mental illness
(including schizophrenia) to recover a better quality of life.

RoSPA (Royal Society for the Prevention of Accidents)
Edgbaston Park
353 Bristol Road
Edgbaston
Birmingham B5 7ST
Tel: 0121 248 2000
Fax: 0121 248 2001
Email: help@rospa.co.uk
Website: www.rospa.com
Advice and publications on preventing accidents.

Royal National Institute of the Blind (RNIB)
105 Judd Street
London WC1H 9NE
Tel: 020 7388 1266
Helpline: 0845 766 9999 (9am–5pm, Mon–Fri)
Fax: 020 7388 2034
Email: helpline@rnib.org.uk
Website: www.rnib.org.uk
Many services for people with visual impairments.

Royal National Institute for Deaf People (RNID)
19–23 Featherstone Street
London EC1Y 8SL
Tel: (switchboard) 020 7296 8000
Textphone Informationline: 0808 808 9000
Voice informationline: 0808 808 0123
Fax: 020 7296 8021
Email: informationline@rnid.org.uk
Website: www.rnid.org.uk
Largest charity reflecting the needs and interests of deaf and hard of hearing people. It provides and offers information, residential care, communication service, disability and deaf awareness training, RNID Typetalk (telephone relay service), RNID Deafness and Disability Solutions.

Samaritans
Tel: 08457 90 90 90
Textphone: 08457 90 91 92
Confidential emotional support is available by telephone 24 hours a day, 365 days of the year. Also accessible by:
- *Personal visit during the daytime and evening (see your phone book for address of local branch)*
- *Letter: write to Chris, PO Box 9090, Stirling FK8 2SA*
- *Email at jo@samaritans.org*

Scottish Association for Mental Health (SAMH)
Cumbrae House
15 Carlton Place
Glasgow G5 9JP

Tel: 0141 568 7000
Fax: 0141 568 7001
Email: enquiries@samh.org.uk
Website: www.samh.org.uk
Information about services in Scotland for people with mental health problems.

Scottish Council for Voluntary Organisations

The Mansfield, Traquair Centre
15 Mansfield Place
Edinburgh EH3 6BB
Tel: 0131 556 3882
Textphone: 0131 557 6483
Fax: 0131 556 0279
Email: enquiries@scvo.org.uk
Website: www.scvo.org.uk
For information about voluntary organisations and councils for voluntary service in Scotland.

Society of Homeopaths

11 Brookfield
Duncan Close
Moulton Park
Northampton NN3 6WL
Tel: 0845 450 6611
Fax: 0845 450 6622
Email: info@homeopathy-soh.org
Website: www.homeopathy-soh.org
For a list of homeopathic practitioners.

Speakability

1 Royal Street
London SE1 7LL
Helpline: 0808 808 9572 (10am–4pm, Mon–Fri)
Publications: 020 7261 9572
Fax: 020 7928 9542
Email: speakability@speakability.org.uk
Website: www.speakability.org.uk
National charity offering information, support and advice for dysphasic adults (loss of language) and their families.

255

Stroke Association
Stroke House
240 City Road
London EC1V 2PR
Helpline: 0845 30 33 100 (9am–5pm, Mon–Fri)
Fax: 020 7490 2686
Email: stroke@stroke.org.uk
Website: www.stroke.org.uk
*Information if you are caring for someone who has had a stroke.
See also Chest, Heart and Stroke Scotland and Chest, Heart and
Stroke Association (Northern Ireland)*

Tripscope
Vassall Centre
Gill Avenue
Bristol BS16 2QQ
Tel: 0117 939 7783
Helpline: 08567 585641 (9am–5pm, Mon–Fri)
Fax: 0117 939 7736
Email: enquiries@tripscope.org.uk
Website: www.tripscope.org.uk
*Information about travel for older and disabled people in the UK and
abroad.*

United Kingdom Home Care Association (UKHCA)
42b Banstead Road
Carshalton Beeches
Surrey SM5 3NW
Tel: 020 8288 1551 (9am–5pm, Mon–Fri)
Fax: 020 8288 1550
Email: enquiries@ukhca.co.uk
Website: www.ukhca.co.uk.
*An association of providers of care at home, with a code of practice. Lists
available of member agencies and others in the UK. Also has information
packs for individuals contracting with independent care agencies.*

Women's Royal Voluntary Service (WRVS)

Milton Hill House
Milton Hill
Abingdon
Oxfordshire OX13 6AD
Tel: 01235 442900
Helpline: 0845 601 4670
Fax: 01235 861166
Email: enquiries@wrvs.org.uk
Website: www.wrvs.org.uk.
A nationwide network of community services, consisting of 115,000 volunteers, including men.

Working Families

1–3 Berry Street
London EC1V 0AA
Tel: 020 7253 7243
Fax: 020 7253 6253
Email: office@workingfamilies.org.uk
Website: www.workingfamilies.org.uk
Helps working parents, children, carers and employers to find a better balance between responsibility at home and at work, with pragmatic advice and practical solutions.

References and further reading

References

Carers UK (2002) *Without us ...? Calculating the value of carers' support*, CUK, London

'Facts about Carers' July *Adding Value: carers as drivers of social change*

General Household Survey (2000) Office of National Statistics, London

Howard, Marilyn (2001) *Paying the Price: carers, poverty and social exclusion*, Child Poverty Action Group (CPAG) and Carers UK, London

HSC 2003/009:LAC(2003)21 (24.09.03) Community Care (delayed discharge) Act 2003 Guidance for Implementation

Lay, Chris and Woods, Bob *Caring for the Person with Dementia: a guide for families and other carers*, Alzheimer's Disease Society, London

Sobczak, Julie (2001) *Alive and Kicking: the carer's guide to exercises for older people*, Age Concern, London

Further reading

Age Concern England and Carers UK publish a wide range of books, factsheets and leaflets that you might find useful. Some of them are listed below; other Age Concern books are listed on pages 264–266.

Age Concern England

Nutritional Care for Older People: A guide to good practice
June Copeman

This book is designed to be used by all care staff concerned with food, nutrition and older people. Drawing on national guidelines, accepted practice and the latest scientific knowledge, this book will help staff develop and maintain the very best standards in all aspects of food management. Topics covered include:

- Food environment
- A–Z checklist of risk factors
- Frequency of meals and fluid intake
- Stimulating a small appetite
- Food and mental health issues
- Cultural and religious issues
- Menu planning and recipes
- Nutritional needs of people with specific illnesses

£14.99 0-86242-284-1

Your Taxes and Savings: A Guide for Older People
Published annually
Paul Lewis

Explains how the tax system affects older people over retirement age, including how to avoid paying more than necessary. The information about savings and investments covers the wide range of opportunities now available and is updated annually.

For further information please telephone 0870 44 22 120.

Factsheets include

2 *Buying retirement housing*
5 *Dental care and older people*
7 *Making your will*
10 *Local authority charging procedures for care homes*

Information on how to obtain Factsheets is given on page 268.

Carers UK

Benefits: what's available and how to get them
Carers Allowance and the Carer Premium
Carers at Work
Children and Young People who have Caring Responsibilities
Direct Payments
Disability Living Allowance and Attendance Allowance
How do I get help?
Juggling Work and Care

Other publications

Buckman, Rob (1988) *I Don't Know What to Say*, published by Papermac, London

Cassar S, Cheney, J and Steed, R (1999) *Safer Handling of People in the Community*, published by BackCare, London

Department of Health (1994) *The Hospital Discharge Workbook*, published by DoH, London [No longer current but still informative.]

A Helping Hand for Benefits (GL21) is available from your local office of the Department for Work and Pensions

King's Fund (1998) *Home from Home*, published by King's Fund, London

Office of Fair Trading (1998) *Older People as Consumers in Care Homes*, published by OFT, London

About Carers UK

Carers UK provides free advice and information to all carers – and runs a network of local branches, where carers can access support or meet other people in a similar position. We also work closely with professionals who work with carers – and support over 800 local organisations, such as carers' centres and projects.

Carers UK's track record in achieving change for carers is second to none. Our research has identified the problems; our policies have suggested solutions; our campaigns have persuaded successive governments to adopt them.

Our work involves:

- reaching out to 'hidden' carers who are unaware of the help available, through our branches and network of local carers' organisations;
- informing carers of their rights through CarersLine (a freephone helpline), our website and leaflets;
- publishing *Caring* – a magazine for members and supporters, which contains news, information, campaign updates and features of general interest to carers;
- researching the problems facing carers, and seeking solutions;
- campaigning to raise awareness of the needs of carers and to encourage action to support them;
- training professionals who work with carers;
- working with business, government and voluntary organisations to overcome barriers to employment for carers who wish to combine paid work with caring;
- involving carers in all its work.

Carers UK

20–25 Glasshouse Yard
London EC1A 4JT
Tel: 020 7490 8818
Email: info@ukcarers.org
CarersLine: 0808 808 7777 (Wed–Thurs, 10am–noon, 2–4pm)
Textphone: 020 7251 8969
Membership hotline: 020 7566 7602
Website: www.carersonline.org.uk

Carers Scotland

91 Mitchell Street
Glasgow
G1 3LN
Tel: 0141 221 9141
Email: info@carerscotland.org

Carers Northern Ireland

58 Howard Street
Belfast BT1 6PJ
Tel: 028 9043 9843
Email: info@carersni.demon.co.uk

Carers Wales

River House
Ynysbridge Court
Gwaelod-y-Garth
Cardiff CF15 9SS
Tel: 029 2081 1370
Email: info@carerswales.org.uk

About Age Concern

Caring for someone in their own home is one of a wide range of publications produced by Age Concern England, the National Council on Ageing. Age Concern works on behalf of all older people and believes later life should be fulfilling and enjoyable. For too many this is impossible. As the leading charitable movement in the UK concerned with ageing and older people, Age Concern finds effective ways to change that situation.

Where possible, we enable older people to solve problems themselves, providing as much or as little support as they need. A network of local Age Concerns, supported by many thousands of volunteers, provides community-based services such as lunch clubs, day centres and home visiting.

Nationally, we take a lead role in campaigning, parliamentary work, policy analysis, research, specialist information and advice provision, and publishing. Innovative programmes promote healthier lifestyles and provide older people with opportunities to give the experience of a lifetime back to their communities.

Age Concern is dependent on donations, covenants and legacies.

Age Concern England
1268 London Road
London SW16 4ER
Tel: 020 8765 7200
Fax: 020 8765 7211
Website: www.ageconcern.org.uk

Age Concern Scotland
113 Rose Street
Edinburgh EH2 3DT
Tel: 0131 220 3345
Fax: 0131 220 2779
Website:
www.ageconcernscotland.org.uk

Age Concern Cymru
4th Floor
1 Cathedral Road
Cardiff CF11 9SD
Tel: 029 2037 1566
Fax: 029 2039 9562
Website:www.accymru.org.uk

Age Concern Northern Ireland
3 Lower Crescent
Belfast BT7 1NR
Tel: 028 9024 5729
Fax: 028 9023 5497
Website: www.ageconcernni.org

Publications from Age Concern Books

Your Rights: A guide to money benefits for older people

Sally West

A highly acclaimed annual guide to the state benefits available to older people. It contains current information on Income Support, Housing Benefit and retirement pensions, among other matters, and provides advice on how to claim.

For more information, please telephone 0870 44 22 120

Housing Options for Older People

Louise Russell

Although not everyone either wants or needs to move just because they reach retirement age, some people will want to move and, for others, circumstances may arise which mean that they may have to move. This book aims to look at all the options open to older people (including staying put), and provides a realistic indication of how easy or difficult each option might be to pursue successfully. Topics covered include:

- whether to stay home or move
- living with relatives or friends
- what type of housing is required
- paying for repairs and improvements
- options for people with limited capital
- other options for homeowners
- your rights if you are a tenant
- ways of adapting your home
- buying or renting accommodation.

Written in straightforward language, this book will help readers to make well-informed decisions about their housing in retirement.

£6.99 0-86242-287-6

Other books in this series

The Carers Handbook series has been written for the carers, families and friends of older people. It guides readers through key care situations and aims to help them make informed, practical decisions. All the books in the series:

- offer step-by-step guidance on the decisions that need to be taken;
- examine all the options available;
- include practical checklists and case studies;
- point you towards specialist help;
- guide you through the social services maze;
- help you to draft a personal plan of action;
- are fully up to date with recent guidelines and issues;
- draw on Age Concern's wealth of experience.

Already published

Caring for someone with depression
Toni Battison
£6.99 0-86242-389-9

Caring for someone with cancer
Toni Battison
£6.99 0-86242-382-1

Caring for someone with a sight problem
Marina Lewycka
£6.99 0-86242-381-3

Caring for someone with a heart problem
Toni Battison
£6.99 0-86242-371-6

Caring for someone with arthritis
Jim Pollard
£6.99 0-86242-373-2

Caring for someone with hearing loss
Marina Lewycka
£6.99 0-86242-380-5

Caring for someone with diabetes
Marina Lewycka
£6.99 0-86242-374-0

Caring for someone who has had a stroke
Philip Coyne with Penny Mares
£6.99 0-86242-369-4

Caring for someone who is dying
Penny Mares
£6.99 0-86242-370-8

Caring for someone with an alcohol problem
Mike Ward
£6.99 0-86242-372-4

Caring for someone at a distance
Julie Spencer-Cingöz
£6.99 0-86242-367-8

The Carers Handbook: What to do and who to turn to
Marina Lewycka
£6.99 0-86242-366-X

Choices for the carer of an elderly relative
Marina Lewycka
£6.99 0-86242-375-9

Caring for someone with dementia
Janie Brotchie
£6.99 0-86242-368-6

If you would like to order any of these titles, please write to the address below, enclosing a cheque or money order for the appropriate amount (plus £1.99 p&p for one book; for additional books please add 75p per book up to a maximum of £7.50) made payable to Age Concern England. Credit card orders may be made on 0870 44 22 120. Books can also be ordered online at www.ageconcern.org.uk/shop

Age Concern Books
Units 5 & 6
Industrial Estate
Brecon
Powys LD3 8LA

Bulk order discounts

Age Concern Books is pleased to offer a discount on orders totalling 50 or more copies of the same title. For details, please contact Age Concern Books on 0870 44 22 120.

Customised editions

Age Concern Books is pleased to offer a free 'customisation' service for anyone wishing to purchase 500 or more copies of the title. This gives you the option to have a unique front cover design featuring your organisation's logo and corporate colours, or adding your logo to the current cover design. You can also insert an additional four pages of text for a small additional fee. Existing clients include many of the biggest names in British industry, retailing and finance, the trades unions, educational establishments, the statutory and voluntary sectors, and welfare associations. **For full details, please contact Sue Henning, Age Concern Books, Astral House, 1268 London Road, London SW16 4ER. Fax: 020 8765 7211. Email: hennins@ace.org.uk**

Visit our Website at www.ageconcern.org.uk/shop

Age Concern Information Line/ Factsheets subscription

Age Concern produces more than 40 comprehensive factsheets designed to answer many of the questions older people (or those advising them) may have. Topics covered include money and benefits, health, community care, leisure and education, and housing. For up to five free factsheets, telephone 0800 00 99 66 (7am–7pm, seven days a week, every day of the year). Alternatively you may prefer to write to Age Concern, FREEPOST (SWB 30375), ASHBURTON, Devon TQ13 7ZZ.

For professionals working with older people, the factsheets are available on an annual subscription service, which includes updates throughout the year. For further details and costs of the subscription, please write to Age Concern England at the above Freepost address.

We hope that this publication has been useful to you. If so, we would very much like to hear from you. Alternatively, if you feel that we could add or change anything, please write and tell us, using the following Freepost address: Age Concern, FREEPOST CN1794, London SW16 4BR

Index